To my parents thank you for always believing in me
and for your ongoing support and love.

To my beautiful husband Ian, thank you for seeing
the potential in me from the day we met and your
ongoing support and love.

To my two beautiful nieces, Evelyn and Lillian.
I wrote this for you both to believe in yourselves
and follow your dreams.

# INTRODUCTiON

Before you begin reading this book and embark on this journey that we take together, I want to share with you quickly why I wrote this book.

My dream of becoming a world-class tennis player began when I was seven years old—when I discovered I was pretty good at it—and continued until I was playing on the European tennis circuit as a nineteen-year-old. I had plenty of support from friends and family but having lost a few matches in that tough environment and living far away from home, self-doubt crept in.

Lacking self-confidence, money and basically not having the psychological skills required to reach the next level, I soon found myself on a plane travelling back to Australia with my dreams a distant memory.

I have since enjoyed an amazing career as a coach in tennis and golf (I will explain about that later) and have taught students from beginner to elite levels. As a coach I have been able to pinpoint many of the pitfalls my clients face that I also fell into as a young tennis player.

The challenges are consistent and easily identified. But if you cannot overcome them you will end up not being able to break through to the next level. It gives me great satisfaction to give my clients, no matter what level they may be at, the tools and support they need to become better players and in many instances, better people.

Of course I wish I had known all this when I was a young tennis player on the verge of breaking through to the next level but I have no regrets. My career has meant that I run a successful business and have travelled to some beautiful parts of the world as a coach. It's given me a comfortable lifestyle and I have met some pretty incredible people along the way.

But I do want to help anyone who reads this book to plan their dream. I will give you the strategies and knowledge to deal with the challenges as they come along.

This is why I have written this book. I have written this book for you. I would love to meet everyone who reads it and am sure I will meet some of you one day. But I hope you will all benefit from the tools I am about to give you. You will become aware of the challenges that lie ahead on your journey and be able to use these strategies to overcome them. You can apply them in your sporting career, in business and in your life.

Think of this book as a blueprint for the person you want to be and for helping you accomplish your ultimate dream. It is interactive, with questions that will unlock parts of you and the reasons why you are on the journey that you have embarked upon. You won't just read this book and say, 'Tiff, that was a good read.'

You will finish it knowing a great deal more about yourself and what you require to accomplish your ultimate dream.

Let's get going on this journey together. I look forward to hearing from you and how this book has helped you get what you want in your life.

Let's make your dream become a reality.

Dream Big, Believe In You and Go After Your Dreams!


Tiffany Mika, February 2019

With thanks to Catherine Zuill for helping write this introduction

# ACKNOWLEDGMENTS

First, I would like to thank Susie Davison for her mentorship and encouragement. She helped me find my true direction and path in life, and I am eternally grateful. Thank you for the guidance and feedback to write this book. Without her, none of this would have been possible.

Thank you to Pat Andersen for introducing Mary Atkins, who gave me the recommendations of which direction to take with this book.

I would like to thank Kaz Williams for getting the ball rolling and start the process of turning this manuscript into the formation of a book.

I would also like to thank Catherine Zuill for meeting with me and helping re-write the introduction to this book.

Thank you to Brian Kannard for his professionalism and helping me forge forward to turning this book into real life.

To my beautiful husband Ian, thank you for always being there, allowing me to grow and develop into the potential you have always seen in me. We are on the journey together, so strap in and enjoy the ride. And thank you for being a huge part of my life.

I can't thank my Mum enough for everything she has done for me. Her love, generosity, ongoing constant support, and always believing I could do anything even when I thought I couldn't. You are an exceptional woman, and I love you dearly.

And thank you to my Dad for always being the provider of our family to give us opportunities to pursue our dreams.

# CHAPTER 1

# GOiNG AFTER YOUR ULTiMATE DREAM

*'A dream doesn't become a reality through magic, it takes sweat, determination and hard work'– Colin Powell*

Do you have a dream? An ultimate dream?

Are you actually living out your dream right now?

Or is it simply something you would love to do, but it's still in your head?

How badly do you want your dream? Seriously, how badly do you really want your dream? I want you to have a think about how important your dream is for you. Are you willing to go after your dream?

My first dream, well, I should say my ultimate dream as a kid and young adult was to become the number-one tennis player in the world.

I can remember as far back as when I was about seven years old when I had my first tennis lesson; I fell ultimately and completely in love. I had always been obsessed with bats and balls from the time I could walk, but standing on that tennis court, at a tennis camp, that was it for me.

I knew what I wanted to do for the rest of my life:

I only wanted to just play tennis!

Has that ever happened to you?

Have you ever found something that you could be completely passionate about, in love with or obsessed about?

Tennis was my passion, my love, my obsession. I lived and breathed it.

My best friend growing up was the brick wall down at the local tennis club. That was where I spent my time growing up, pounding the ball away at the wall, back and forth, day in and day out (well, when I didn't have to go to school).

I would spend the whole weekend at the local tennis courts, with my best friend (the brick wall), playing competitions and living in hope that I could play with other people down there. That was my life. I was madly in love with my life then. It was everything to me. I still look back at those times fondly and have realized how fortunate I was that my mum, especially, encouraged me to play tennis.

We lived next door to a home that had a tennis court. The owners of the tennis court would allow me to play there anytime, and for a kid like me that was a dream come true.

I did have an awesome mum. After school I would be waiting on the bottom steps of our house with two tennis racquets and balls, and when Mum came home from work she would take me to next door's court and play tennis with me.

I loved every second I was on the tennis court. I always felt very much at home on there; it always felt very natural to me and like the place where I belonged. I did play other sports at school as well, and represented the school in many of them as well as tennis. I just loved ball sports. I felt like I had an affinity with a ball.

When finishing Year 12, I was discussing with my parents what I wanted to do with my life, because finally my time at school was over. My mum knew how much I wanted to play tennis. I had grown up in a country town, Grafton the 'Jacaranda City', and there were no opportunities there, so we looked into my other options.

My dad, however, was not keen on the idea of me becoming a tennis player. He said to me, 'I want you to get a real job.' Dad didn't understand my passion for tennis. The way he was brought up was to leave school and get a job, that's all he knew. Dad didn't speak to me for it felt like three weeks, though it could have been three days, or even three hours. I can't really remember the time frame, but Dad had made his point.

We do laugh about it all the time, even now, about me getting a 'real job'. What is a real job anyway? To my dad it was working in an office nine to five, Monday to Friday, but I have never had a real job (well, not for very long—I will share with you shortly how that turned out).

Once I finished school I headed to Brisbane, where I spent the next year of my life at a Tennis Academy, the same one Pat Rafter would attend, where I was training ten hours a day. All my dreams had come true.

After this year at the Academy, I had an opportunity to play tennis in Europe but I didn't have any money to get there. What do you do when you don't have money? Well you get a job. And so that's what I did.

This was where I got a real job, yes you know that nine to five thing that my dad so much wanted me to do. I lasted a month at that job, confined in a cubicle for eight hours a day. I worked with an international banking corporation and in my first month I got a promotion. I guess most people would be excited about it. Not me, I felt too confined, like I was trapped in those four walls. It was like being a caged-in lion and I was just roaring to get out of there. Hence, after a month at that job I left. It was really a means to end anyway because all I wanted to do was to fund my trip to Europe.

I got a job as a car detailer working sixty to seventy hours a week. I did that for about four months to earn enough to support myself in Europe. I figured if I ran out of money I would just find work over there to support my tennis career until I was making money from that. I was nineteen, full of hope and massive dreams.

Looking back I am proud of myself for being determined to make it work: I got a job to support my ultimate dream and travelled overseas alone to pursue a dream. It was an awesome experience for sure. I was totally out of my comfort zone and experiencing new adventures every day. I would recommend that to anyone: get out there and explore the world, don't just settle.

I wasn't winning tennis tournaments, to be honest I wasn't doing very well at all. I struggled to get through the first rounds at most tournaments. Money was running low and consequently I would get gardening and cleaning jobs to support myself so I could buy food and have a roof over my head.

I was pretty much doing it alone. I did start to ask the questions, 'Why am I overseas? Why I am playing tennis?' My game wasn't improving. I was losing every time I stepped onto the court. I was frustrated, I was depressed and my dream of becoming the best tennis player in the world was slipping through my fingers. That's what it felt like. I was losing, there was no improvement, I was repeating the same thing over and over again in every tournament I competed in, and the major problem was I didn't know how to get help.

I thought I had to do it alone! That was what I had learned growing up, that if you want to get anywhere in life you have to do it alone, do not rely on anyone, you are on your own.

What I was not aware of when I was playing these tournaments overseas was that I needed help with the mental part of my game. That was why I was losing matches consistently. I had the physical ability and the talent, but I didn't know how to use my head, how to control my emotions in those pressure situations, or how to maintain focus and not let my mind wander.

After six months of being in Europe I rang my mum and said, 'I'm coming back home to go to university and get a real job.' That was the biggest moment and decision I had made in my life at that time and over the next fourteen years it shaped a person who, when I look back now, I see as a very sad girl.

What I will tell you right now, is that when I made that decision to come back home and go to university, I felt like a failure. I was absolutely devastated. It was like losing my partner in life. I was numb, empty and dead inside. My dream that was my everything was over. It was what I had pursued for my whole childhood and teenage life. It was all I knew.

I remember a time when I returned to Sydney from Europe and I was sitting on a train. I don't remember where I was going, but I remember feeling so sad and devastated that I had lost my one true love. I looked out the window of the train and saw a tennis court. I couldn't bear to look at it. It was just so painful that I turned away.

My heart was completely broken. It felt as though I had a stake pushed deep into it, that it was broken into small pieces never to be mended again. I didn't pick up a tennis racquet for about two years after that. I just couldn't bear it.

At the time I didn't understand what was happening, but I was going through a grieving process.

I felt as if my life was over and I had to find a new life. How could I find a new life? The plan was to be a tennis player and nothing else, absolutely nothing else.

There was no plan B only plan A. So what was I to do?

I will share more of my story later in the book but for now, I have a very important question to ask you:

Are you pursuing your ultimate dream?

If you said, 'Yes, Tiff, I am going after my ultimate dream!' then I say to you right now: GO FOR IT!

But can you do me a favour?

Don't stop reading, this book is for you too, even though you are already working on your dream. The practical steps I can share with you through what I have learned along the way, through sport, business and life will definitely help sort out the questions that will come up for you, plus give you practical steps to take in order to work through the obstacles and, yes, the challenges you will face.

There will be times when you will question whether you should still be pursuing your dream. It's not as easy as people make out, no one told me how hard it was going to be.

I will say, don't you dare give up on you, just keep going. I believe in you, but *you* have to believe in you.

We will discuss your beliefs in another chapter, but right now let's keep talking about your dream.

What if you said to me, 'Tiff, I am not going after my dream. I was told I would never make it. I was told to give up. I was told I was just not good enough.'

Then, my friend, I say to you: What do you really want?

Recently on a television program I was watching, this nineteen-year-old girl was on a train on her way to university. She was observing everyone on the train and she thought, 'They are all living their second choice. I am not going to settle and live my second choice. I want to live my first choice!' She is pursuing her singing career and not settling for anything else.

So I will ask you: Do you want to live your first choice and go after your dream?

Or do you want to live your second choice, third choice, fourth choice and so on?

I want you to shout out as loud as you can: 'I WANT TO LIVE MY FIRST CHOICE!'

Now stand up and shout it out again: 'I WANT TO LIVE MY FIRST CHOICE!'

Just do it one more time: 'I WANT TO LIVE MY FIRST CHOICE!'

OK this is awesome, we have some work to do.

If you are still figuring it out, keep reading, because we can work it all out together.

## MUST YOU HAVE A DREAM?

Some people will refer to having a dream as having a purpose. You may have heard many of the leaders in the personal-development space talking about having a purpose.

What's your purpose this, what's your purpose that?

You know what, you must have a dream! You must have a purpose! You must have a reason to get out of bed in the morning because if you don't, what's the point?

Can you just go along for the rest of your life, going through the motions?

Picture yourself ten years from now, what do you see?

Are you any different? You may not see anything yet. But I will tell you that if you don't have anything to work towards, you will be lost, you will be angry, you will be frustrated. You may even blame everyone around you, your family, your friends, your teachers and anyone else that comes to mind.

Just even thinking about wasting the next ten years of your life, ah, it makes me feel so torn up inside. Life is precious.

When we are young we think, 'Ah, I have lots of time.' But you know what? Time moves so fast. As I am writing this book I am forty-seven years old, nearly forty-eight. I still feel like I have the energy and excitement of an eight-year-old kid, but when I look in the mirror, I see the face and body of a woman who is getting close to fifty. It's a bit of a shock.

I can't remember what has happened to the last thirty years, since I finished school. Where has the time gone?

If you are the same age as me or older I know you get it!

So let's not waste time anymore. Let's get on with it!

## HOW BADLY DO YOU WANT IT?

Yep, that's right, how badly do you really want this dream to come true in your life?

Bad enough that you are willing to do the work?

And what I mean by work is: are you willing to plan it out in detail down to what you need to do each hour to make it happen?

Because that's what it is going to take.

I was reading this book written by Mark Manson, *The Subtle Art of Not Giving a F#ck*, and Mark was talking about how he wanted to be a rock star. Any guitar song he listened to, he could envisage himself on the stage, playing to the screams of the crowd. This would keep him occupied for hours on end.

Mark never questioned whether he would ever be on stage, Mark believed it was just a matter of time. But what he discovered was that he was in love with the dream, he was in love with the result—he didn't want to have to do the work to get there. He realized it was going to take him countless hours of practice, it was going to be a daily grind. He would have to find a group to work with and deal with the logistics involved in rehearsal times, the challenge of finding gigs, then marketing to get people to the gigs and the list continues.

You see and he is the first one to admit it, he didn't want it bad enough.

Do you remember me talking about my tennis dream?

I did want it bad enough. I would grind it out ten hours a day on and off the court. It was a daily slog. But I wanted to do it! I wanted to do the work.

But do you?

Do you really want this dream?

Do you know what it will take?

The first step in pursuing your dream is going to be awareness. It is going to be the awareness of the effort it is going to take. Not just the physical effort. It is going to take everything you have got and more.

You better get strapped in because you are going to go on a hell of a ride.

## IT IS GOiNG TO BE PAiNFUL

I am not going to sugar-coat this for you. As much as I would like to say, 'Oh, it's a journey and you have to enjoy the journey, blah, blah!' the truth is, it is going to be damn painful!

But you know what? It will be worth it. I am constantly telling people that you have to go through the pain to get to the pleasure. That's what it always feels like. It will be tough, but it will be worth it when you get to the other side.

When I was thirty-four, I took up a new sport. It was golf. I was never interested in the sport at all, until my lovely mum bought me a few golf lessons for Christmas.

I thought, 'OK this is going to be interesting. It should be pretty easy this golf thing. Why wouldn't it be? I was an accomplished sportsperson. I had played just about any sport you can think of and represented my school for most of them. I taught tennis through my tennis coaching and sports-skills business for kids. How hard could it be? The ball isn't even moving!

Wrong!

My first thirty-minute golf lesson consisted of lots of air swings, balls running along the ground left and right, not one that went straight, let alone in the air. All the shots were worm burners!

But I had fallen in love. I had found a new sport. I absolutely love striking balls with a club. I love the feeling of hitting a ball.

I love the sound it makes when you hit it sweet in the centre. I love the feeling of hitting an absolutely pure shot. It is effortless and exhilarating at the same time. It's pure ecstasy! You don't need a drug to make you feel this way, it's a natural high.

Even though in that first lesson I struggled to make a connection - and believe you me, I was incredibly frustrated being the sportsperson that I am - reality eventually set in. I was just like everyone else on a level playing field of beginner land. I wanted to prove to myself that I could do it.

So there I was, fallen completely in love with a new sport. I could see a vision of me actually being able to play golf; wow, I could even see myself on the golf tour playing it out with the best of them in the world. But how was I going to get there?

Remember how Mark Manson wanted to be a rock star, but he didn't want the hassle of having to do the work to get there, because it was going to take a lot of time, a lot of effort? Hey, the reality is that even if you do the work you don't know if you are going to get there anyway until you do.

Now we will talk about a plan and how to work out a plan when we get to the last chapter, but I will tell you this now: golf was damn hard to learn. I did manage to get down to a scratch handicap in three years. But I practised twelve hours a day when I wasn't tennis coaching. And when I was working I would get up early and be on the practice range at 5.30 a.m. before my first tennis lesson or sports-skills class at 9 a.m. Any break I had throughout the day I would be back on the golf course, refining my technique, practising until it got dark.

Now, this was just practising. Prior to competitions or tournaments I would warm up for about two hours, play, then head back out for more practising and refinement until it got dark. The coach I had in the early days did warn me that I had to pay my dues on the golf course.

What he meant was that I had to give myself time to learn not only the skills but how to actually play on a golf course. He said, 'You are going to come up against women who will be twice your age, sixty and seventy years of age, and they are going to beat you, and you will hate it.' I said, 'Oh no, I'll be right, I won't hate it.'

You know, he was right!

I hated being beaten by ladies who were older than me. It was so painful to be beaten by players who I thought were not as good as me technically. Even though it was still the very early days of learning for me, I hated it.

It was tough on my ego. But, I had to work through it. It was a painful process, being a beginner at something, not knowing anything and having to go through the same learning as everyone else. I hated that feeling, I was totally out of my comfort zone. But in order for me to become the golfer I wanted to become I knew I had to do the work.

I have taught many ladies golf over the past decade. They all say the same thing to me: I want to be consistent in my golf game. My answer is that they are going to have to do the practice and it is going to be a series of slow progressions and it will be frustrating to learn this game because it is not as simple as just picking up a golf club and off you go.

It will be the same for your dream. You don't just say one day, I want to be this! Then the next day you wake up as the new you. You are going to have to do the work. I want to prepare you for this now right here in Chapter 1. It is going to be hard and you are going to be tested.

But, do you want to live your first choice in life? Or do you want to live your fifth choice, not even your second choice?

I think you know the answer to that.

So let's get to it!

## YOU HAVE TO WANT IT SO BAD TO TAKE ACTiON

When I say that 'you have to want it so bad', you have to want it so bad that it hurts.

If you don't take action on your dream you will regret it for the rest of your life, and that too will hurt. I can share plenty of regrets with you, and I have massive regrets, but I am sure I am not going to get to the end of my life, lying on my death bed, and say, 'Oh I wish I had written that book I always wanted to write.' You know why? Simply because I have done it. You are reading what has been sitting in my head waiting to come out for years.

Do you know what the number-one regret people have towards the end of their lives? It's that they lived someone else's dream and not their own! Now that is painful!

But don't just say one day I will have this or one day I will have that. The cold hard truth is that you won't have it unless you want it bad enough. If you want it, you will go after it and work your butt off to get it.

A few years ago I had a young woman, Georgie, approach me about becoming a professional golfer. She was twenty-seven years old and had played as a junior, but had this nagging feeling that she hadn't gone after her dream. She was working at a job that she quite liked, the hours were long, there were numerous responsibilities she had taken on, but it wasn't what she ideally wanted.

We started working together on her ultimate dream with regular lessons and competitions to get used to playing under pressure. We mapped out a regular practice-and-training regime and we worked together for about six months—her handicap was dropping dramatically, she was performing well, she was on target. But something happened. I can't be sure why, but she stopped pursuing her dream. I suspect that her workload for this dream was tough, as she was holding down a full-time job, and perhaps the pressure of the job won.

I don't know. But what I can tell you is there was a lot going on in her life: a full-time job, a relationship, plus there was no guarantee she was going to make it. Quite possibly she didn't have enough confidence in herself to believe she could get there. She may have just settled for where she was in her job. It may have given her the security that she wanted, whereas there was no security, no certainty that she was going to make it as a professional athlete and achieve her ultimate dream.

But you don't know if you are going to get there, until you are there.

*Don't live with regret. It will eat you up inside.*

So let's work through this together right now so that you don't have any regrets and you know you have given your all.

Before we begin, I'd like you to have a dedicated journal to use alongside this book, as I am going to pose many questions that I want you to answer as we go. This is not a book that you are going to read and then put back on the shelf; it is going to be the book that will give you the action steps that you will need to take to go after that ultimate dream we have been talking about.

We have to get it out of your head and onto paper. You need to see it, you need to write it, you need to feel the emotions through your body as you write it.

Let's begin.

## QUESTiONS ABOUT YOUR DREAM

1. *What is your ultimate dream?*

   Write in detail your ultimate vision. Who are you? What are you doing? Where are you? Get it down, in detail, and out of your head.

2. *Why do you want this ultimate dream?*

   Answer in detail why you want this ultimate dream and how important it is for you.

3. *Who is it that you are pursuing this ultimate dream for?*

   Are you working towards this dream for yourself or for someone else?

4. *If for yourself, why for you?*

   If for someone else, why for them?

5. *If for you, explain in detail why you want to do it for you?*

   If for someone else, explain in detail why you want to do it for someone else?

OK great, we have established your ultimate dream, why you want it and who you are doing it for, whether it be you or someone else.

Now let's get a little deeper.

Let's tap into why you want to do this so badly. We want to get to the core of what it is that will drive you. Unless we understand what will drive you and your reasoning behind it all, it won't be enough just wanting the dream to come true and you won't work on achieving it.

# THE 7 LEVEL WHYS

## WHAT ARE THE 7 LEVEL WHYS?

The 7 level whys are very powerful as they help identify how you think and feel at your core about what you are about to embark on.

I discovered this questioning through a book I read called *Millionaire Success Habits* by Dean Graziozi.

When I did this questioning of myself, it really uncovered that at my core I felt like I wasn't good enough. And that this feeling stemmed back to when I was playing a tennis tournament when I was about ten years old. I remember it clearly. I said to myself, 'What if I give it my all, I try as hard as I can and I still lose? It will prove that I am not good enough!'

I carried that feeling deep in my core from that moment. I wasn't aware of what I was instilling at the time. How are you supposed to know that when you are a kid? But, from that moment, it did affect every decision I made at a subconscious level.

When I did lose tennis matches I could justify losing by saying, 'that I didn't try. That's why I lost.' But really what was happening deep within, was that I was terrified of losing. If I lost that meant I was a failure. If I was a failure, then I wasn't good enough. And little did I know at the time that I was planting a seed that would hold me back from everything I wanted in my life.

In hindsight, I actually achieved quite a lot. I represented the school in every sports team that I tried out for. I had the opportunity to play professional tennis, I got a university degree, established three successful businesses, became a qualified tennis, sport and golf coach, plus played golf off scratch. I achieved all of that with a deep-seated belief that I wasn't good enough. Imagine what I would have accomplished had I believed I was good enough?

## YOUR 7 LEVEL WHYS

It's time to get out that journal to work through this exercise.

1.  Ask yourself 'Why do I want to achieve this ultimate dream?' Write down your answer.

2.  With your answer you will find reasons why you want to achieve this dream. With those reasons, ask yourself the question: Why?

3.  Each time you explain the reasons why, ask the question again. Why? Do this until you have asked the question—why?—seven times!

Here's an example.

*Why do I want to achieve this ultimate dream?*

My ultimate dream is to have an academy that is designed to help young girls, teenage girls and women achieve their goals and dreams. It will help them to work on their mindset and show them that nothing can ever hold them back. It will be designed to show them the steps and the systems that they need in place to go after their ultimate goal in life.

*Why?*

I want to do this because I know what it is like to not know how to get that dream you so badly want. Over the years I have learned systems and structures, plus I have the life experience, to teach others how to get there. It is really important to me to guide my nieces through their lives too, so they can grow up to be confident women.

*Why?*

Because I wish I'd had someone to show me the way when I was a teenager. To show me how to set goals, how to reverse engineer them, how to structure my days to set myself up for success, what type of questions to ask myself, how to control my emotions and what to do when I hit a wall (barrier).

*Why?*

I felt very lost and frustrated as a teenager and as an adult. I didn't achieve my ultimate dream and just fell into things along the way. I felt as if I was always trying to re-invent myself into something else because I had let myself down.

*Why?*

I had let myself down because I didn't achieve my dream of becoming the number-one tennis player in the world.

*Why?*

I didn't become the number-one tennis player in the world because I didn't try hard enough to figure out how to get there.

*Why?*

Because I didn't believe in myself and I thought I wasn't good enough.

There you go, this is an example but a true example. My original inability to achieve my dream came back to not believing in me, believing I was not good enough. Therefore, any decisions made from that moment always had at their foundation the idea that I was not good enough.

Now it's your turn!

Do the '7 Level Whys' exercise before we continue.

Welcome back!

How did you go?

What came up for you?

Now that we have gone deeper into your core in order for you to understand yourself better and what decisions you are going to make from this point forward.

Once you understand what is much deeper inside, you are more aware. Once you are more aware, you will make better decisions. Once you make better deciions, you will have better results. Once you have better results, there will be no stopping you and nothing will hold you back!

*Awareness = Better Results.*

# CHAPTER 2

# BELiEVE IN YOU, TRUST YOU!

'Keep your dreams alive. Understand to achieve anything requires
faith and belief in yourself, vision, hard work, determination,
and dedication.' – Gail Devers

Do you believe in *you*?

This is a very serious question. I ask you this at the beginning of this chapter because if you do not believe in you and you do not trust you, if you doubt yourself, you won't achieve your ultimate dream.

This is reality. I would consider that the most important thing for any sportsperson, businessperson or really anyone that has a dream that they want to achieve in life, is to believe in themselves!

## WHAT IS BELiEVING IN YOU?

This is having the belief that you can do anything no matter what is thrown at you—curve balls, brick walls, barriers, challenges—and that you can work through it to achieve your dreams.

I will share with you what happened when I had no belief in me, no trust in my decisions and no self-esteem.

I was eighteen years old. I had finished school and moved to a tennis academy where I could pursue my tennis career. I was working my butt off to become a professional tennis player. I mentioned this in the first chapter: it was my ultimate dream. That was it, nothing else, just a professional tennis player. I was very clear on my dream.

However, there was a problem. Turned out to be a major one at that! I had no belief in myself, nothing, zilch! I never trusted decisions that I had made. It's a wonder that I still won tennis tournaments in my junior years, because if you had asked me to rate my belief in myself on a belief monitor, with 10 being the highest and 1 being the lowest, I would have rated myself at about a minus 2!

I purely relied on my athletic skills and the amount of training that I applied on a daily basis to get me through. However, when I was coming up against low-ranked professionals on the tour, I would get absolutely smashed! It was humiliating.

I didn't know it was my lack of belief that was causing many of the losses or it was my mindset holding me back. I thought it was the fact that I just didn't work hard enough. I would head back out on the court and drill even harder the next day, train even harder in sprints, work even harder in the gym.

I thought that I should 'just know' how to work through it, and physically work hard I did, but no one told me I had to really work on me; my mindset, my belief systems, my emotions—there was no suggestion of the kind. It was just drill harder from the coaches, and if you lost in pressure points in training, then you just did push ups. I became very strong that year, many push ups, but became worse in tournament performances and on-court skills training.

I still remember this one particular tournament I played where I was drawn to play a well-known Australian player in the first round. She was ranked as one of the top Australian players at the time.

I was so nervous I couldn't think straight, my arms and legs felt really heavy, like when you get the flu and your body aches, your legs feeling so heavy that you struggle to walk up stairs panting: that was how I felt. My mind was going a million miles an hour. I knew I had done the physical work, but I was so frightened that I would make a mistake and humiliate myself, that that was exactly what happened.

I could barely hit a ball over the net in the warm-up. I struggled to move to the ball, my legs just couldn't get there. Now this was the warm-up. You can imagine what was going to happen in the match. If I were someone watching on the sidelines, I would have covered my eyes with my hands and not even peeked through the fingers to have the odd glance.

We began the match. My opponent served first and I hit every return out of the court. Not one return over the net and into the court to give me a fighting chance, all the balls went out. Then it was my turn to serve. This was the second game and we had changed ends. I managed to get my serves over the net and into the service box, but then each return would go bang, straight past me down the line, or bang, straight past me cross court.

Can you imagine what was going on in my head? Here I was, my belief in myself was a minus 2 and I was trying not to be humiliated. Thoughts were running through my mind, 'Tiff, you are having yourself on', 'Tiff, I told you, you can't play tennis', 'Tiff, you have got no hope of becoming a pro tennis player', 'Who do you think you are Tiff? You have got no hope!'

Every time I made a mistake, hit the ball into the net or out, got passed at the net, winners returned down the line and cross court off my serve, I kept telling myself, 'You are having yourself on Tiff!'

I had lost the first set convincingly 6–0 and it was my serve to start the next set. I lost my service game, we changed ends, then I got ready to serve again. Now this will tell you my state of mind in that moment. My opponent said, 'What are you doing? You just served the last game!'

You know I couldn't remember serving the last game, I had no recollection of it. I was in such a state of self-destruction, I was not in the game at all. You know that saying, 'the lights are on but no one is at home', well that day, there were no lights on and definitely no one was at home.

Guess what the score was for that match? Yes, you are right, it was 6–0 6–0. I felt so humiliated, so devastated, so disgusted, I went and hid somewhere safe behind the clubhouse so no one could see and bawled my eyes out. It was uncontrollable crying! No one saw me, luckily no one heard me, but, looking back, it seemed to be a turning point for me where I made a decision about my life and my future as a tennis player.

Years later, when I was about thirty-five years old, I attended a personal development course. I had begun to learn and play golf. I saw golf as my second chance to become the professional athlete I had always wanted to become. The reason I went to this course was that my tennis demons were coming back to haunt me and I didn't want to repeat history. I was more mature and wise enough to realize that I needed to work on me.

In this particular course I attended, the course instructor said that there are significant events that happen in our lives, and these significant events are when we make decisions about the world. To give you an idea it's usually around the ages of four to six when we make our first decision about the world: something significant happens and we make a decision about life. Then when we are in our pre-pubescent years, say ten to twelve years old, we make another decision about the world, and then, when we are in early adulthood, around eighteen to twenty-one years old, we make yet another decision about the world.

These three significant decisions are what shape us into the people we become as an adults.

If we refer back to that tennis tournament where I felt humiliated, devastated and was telling myself right through that match that I was 'no good', I was at one of those ages of making a decision about the world. I was eighteen or nineteen then. I kept telling myself I was no good, and I made the decision then that 'I wasn't good enough!'

It wouldn't matter in the future how hard I worked at pursuing my tennis career (which I only pursued for another year after that), I would keep telling myself 'I wasn't good enough.'

I carried that feeling right through until the age of thirty-five, some fifteen years later, until I discovered what it was that was holding me back from going after my dream.

I tell you this story because I don't want you to waste precious years believing that you can't achieve anything you want in your life.

It took me thirty-five years to wake up and become aware of what was going on in my world. When I look back, no wonder I didn't make it as a professional tennis player. No wonder I attracted the wrong people into my life. No wonder I just settled for second, third or fourth best. No wonder I put everyone else before me.

I didn't believe I was worth it!

In the 1960s there was a book released called *Psycho-Cybernetics* by Dr Maxwell Maltz. Dr Maltz, a plastic surgeon, would do facial reconstructions for people who thought they were unattractive. What Maltz discovered was that even though he would give the patients what they wanted, they were still unhappy. They had poor self-image.

What did Maltz do? He worked on improving their self-belief.

You can have all the coaching, attend all the seminars, webinars, trainings, live events and work your butt off, but, at the end of the day, if you do not BELIEVE IN YOU then, my friend, you won't reach your dreams and your goals.

Ask any successful businessperson or sportsperson. They will all tell you that is the number-one element for success. You must have ultimate belief in yourself and ultimate belief in what you are pursuing.

You can have what you want but you must be willing to go to work on you!

David J. Schwartz who wrote *The Magic of Thinking Big* says, 'Believe it can be done. When you believe something can be done, really believe, your mind will find the ways to do it. Believing a solution paves the way to solution.'

When you are starting out, you don't know if your plans are going to work. You have a goal for your business or a goal for your sporting dream, but there is no proof that it will succeed. Well, not for you, because you haven't achieved it yet. But if there is doubt in whether you can do this, then this will be the number-one reason that will hold you back.

It was like me wanting to be the number-one tennis player in the world. I didn't know if I was going to succeed, but it was all I wanted. I had the skills, the talent, the determination, the focus and work ethic in place, it was all there.

But the most essential element was missing.

There was no belief in myself. I did not believe in me, and my negative thoughts about me affected every single decision I made. Not that I was aware of it at the time.

When I started my sports-skills and tennis-coaching business after I finished university I didn't know if the business was going to work. There were plenty of tennis coaches around and we all did the same thing: we all taught tennis.

In order for my business to stand out I had to get out of the 'sea of sameness' and not be like all the other tennis coaches. I saw a gap in the marketplace, it was an opportunity to be unique. No other tennis coaches were teaching sports skills on a tennis court, especially to the younger kids, the three- to five-year-olds. There was my point of difference.

The point I am making here is that I didn't know if my business was going to work. I had to believe that what I was doing was going to make a difference and have an impact on children's sports development and social development.

It was the same when I moved into the golf industry. How did I know that my golf business would work? I didn't know. I had to believe that if I could be different to all

the other golf coaches, offer a point of difference, be unique and specialize in an area that most golf coaches weren't offering, I could create a captive audience.

## WHAT WILL HAPPEN IF YOU WON'T BELIEVE IN YOU?

Let's talk about you.

We talked about going after your ultimate dream in the first chapter and here I am now asking you what will happen if you won't believe in you?

Really what will happen?

You heard my story about my complete lack of belief in me, but what about you?

I am going to ask again, 'What Will Happen If You Won't Believe In You?'

I can tell you what will happen. You won't achieve your big-ass dream that's what!

You will be angry, frustrated, possibly aggressive, depressed, devastated, alone and no one will understand how you are feeling. They won't get it. It will affect how you treat yourself and how you treat people around you; you won't have any respect for anyone, because you have lost respect for yourself. You will attract people who will control you, tell you what to do, put you down, bully you and of course you will believe everything they say, because why would you be right? You will always see yourself as wrong. You won't go after anything or push yourself, you will just fall into whatever comes along, because you will be lost, everything that you ever wanted is no longer there on your path, because you gave up on you.

That's right! You gave up on you!

Get out your journal and write out the question:

*What Will Happen If I Don't Believe In Me?*

I want you to understand and to become aware that if you don't believe in you, you are going to miss out and live life with regret.

It took me until the age of forty-five to come to terms with never being the tennis player I wanted to be. I was at an online-marketing event in Thailand and I was listening to a speaker on the subject of belief and lack of belief.

Something went off inside and I cried for two hours straight. I realized I had been holding on to this feeling of a lack of accomplishment since I was twenty years old. That's when I gave up on my tennis career and gave up on me. It was deep-seated, as you can imagine. But it was the release I needed in order to move forward.

Don't hold back on you. You are worth it!

Now answer that question before we continue.

I will remind you again here, write out this question and answer it:

*What Will Happen If I Don't Believe In Me?*

OK so now you have answered that question.

What have you discovered if you won't or don't believe in you?

## HOW WOULD YOU RATE YOUR BELiEF IN YOU?

How would you rate your belief in you today? If 10 was rated as the highest, where you have ultimate belief in your abilities, and 1 is the lowest, where you have no belief whatsoever, how would you rate yourself?

If you scored 10, congratulations, you are half way there towards achieving your dream. There will be more to do than just having a high-quality belief system, but this is awesome because you will not question yourself when times get tough, when it becomes challenging and you are tested. You will have the strength to be able to work through it. Congratulations.

If you scored less than 10, then we have some work to do.

## HOW TO GET YOUR BELIEF SYSTEM UP TO 10!

Do you remember in the last chapter we discussed your 7 Level Whys?

What did you discover about you?

Did you discover what was holding you back?

With mine it was about not being good enough. As we discussed, every decision that was made from that point forward was about not being good enough.

But how can we turn that around, to believing that you are good enough and that you can achieve anything you want to achieve?

It's about developing standards for how you believe you should show up in the world. What you expect from yourself. This will build confidence in you and when you are confident and you believe in you—NOTHING WILL STOP YOU!

It's time to establish your new set of standards now.

## TAKE CONTROL OF YOUR EMOTIONS

You have to take control of your emotions!

*We control our emotions* rather than have our emotions controlling us.

Playing sport offers great examples. When we play sport we can get very emotional about our performance on the court, the field, the golf course, whatever your chosen domain. We get emotional because we care. We want to do well, we want to feel good, we love being out there playing and competing.

However, we will be challenged when we are on the field.

Remember that tennis tournament I mentioned and how humiliated I felt. I had all these thoughts running through my mind, telling me I wasn't good enough, that I was hopeless and so on. You can only imagine the emotions I was going through. I was upset, frustrated, angry and confused. I was letting all of this happen to me. I was right in the middle of a meltdown and didn't know what to do about it.

I distinctly remember another meltdown I had when I was playing golf. I had got down to a 10 handicap after playing for two years and was about to play a local golf competition with a seventeen-year-old girl who played off scratch. Watch out, my tennis demons were coming back to haunt me! I felt inadequate and I didn't like the environment I was in. I was always playing with the girl's mother and she carried on and on like competitive parents do in sport. It took me back to my tennis days.

All I did throughout that game was tell myself how bad I was, that I wasn't good enough, that I was having myself on. Does it sound familiar? You can see there is a pattern. Different sport but same reaction. This occurred all because I couldn't control my emotions; not only couldn't control them, I didn't know how to control them. I didn't know I could.

Rather than let the tennis demons revisit, it was time to make a change.

You see, if you don't learn how to control your emotions and how to respond to situations that come up for you, you will always revert back to the same old patterns. Basically they are habits.

A habit is a routine of behaviour that is repeated regularly and tends to occur subconsciously, which means we are not aware that it occurs. It's just what we do. A lot of what we do and how we react is what we learn as we grow up. We learn it from our parents, our teachers, our peers and anyone else that has an impact on us.

Are the habits we learn as kids good? Sure some habits can be fantastic, but others can be detrimental. I am not blaming parents, teachers, peers or anyone else of influence, as they have learned their habits the same way through the previous generations. However, what we want to do here is to become aware of our habits. What we need to do in this section is to become aware of our emotions.

This is the process of how we operate on an emotional level.

*T. F. A. R.*

*T = Thoughts*

*F = Feelings*

*A = Actions*

*R = Results*

*Thoughts ➤ Feelings ➤ Actions ➤ Results*

## THOUGHTS

Our thoughts are what we think about and therefore we believe they are real. They become our beliefs, our reality, what we believe in our world. Therefore, how we think and what we believe will create our feelings.

## FEELINGS

Our feelings are our emotions. They are how we feel about what we have decided to think about, what our beliefs are. Therefore we will feel what we believe. Our emotions have a huge range from happy and excited to sad and depressed. What we believe is how we will then feel.

## ACTIONS

Our actions are what then happen after we have decided on a thought or a belief about something, then we have backed it up with an emotion to go with that belief.

This will then lead to an action that is, in fact, a reaction to that belief and the emotion that goes with it.

## RESULTS

The is the fourth step of the process. It will give us the final result or outcome of what we thought, how we felt, and the action we took to give us the result.

Let's look at that tennis match that haunted me for years.

Thoughts: I thought I was having myself on, I wasn't good enough, I was kidding myself.

Feelings: It brought up anger, frustration, tears.

Actions: Hitting balls out of the court constantly, couldn't move to the ball, couldn't focus on the game.

Results: Lost the match

◎

Now it's your turn. Was there a time when you went through something similar?

In your journal, write out T.F.A.R. and an event that happened to you that had a negative result.

◎

OK! Now let's look at something awesome that happened.

I will give you an example of a time when I played my best golf.

Thoughts: No thoughts, my head was clear, my mind was empty.

Feelings: It brought up ultimate confidence and a feeling of flow and being in the zone. I felt invincible.

Actions: Hitting the ball wherever I wanted. Everything was easy. My swing rhythm was smooth.

Results: Played my best golf, won a tournament.

◎

I am not saying that every time you go through this process you will win a tournament. You may not, but you will have feel as though you have achieved your best.

Now your turn. Was there a time when you went through something similar?

In your journal, write out T.F.A.R. and an event that happened to you that had a positive result.

◎

So you can see what happens when you go through this process.

Now these were more reactions though, weren't they? You were just identifying how the process works with a positive or negative thought.

What if you could control it?

Would it improve your performance on the court, the field, the golf course, in the boardroom, in your business?

Of course it would.

But how do you do it?

We will get to that in the steps following.

## STEPS TO CONTROLLING YOUR EMOTIONS

### STEP 1: EVIDENCE JOURNAL

I discovered Evidence Journals this year, a few weeks before I started writing this book. I was attending a women's networking morning tea and the speaker of the day was talking about an Evidence Journal.

In an Evidence Journal, you make a statement about yourself for the day, and this helps you see evidence from the universe throughout the day that proves how you show up in the world. It's amazing what it can do to help you realize how great you really are both in life and with the people around you.

For example, write today's date in your journal, and then state how you are going to show up in the world. Let's say that you write, 'I am strong!' Now throughout the day you will see things come up for you that make you more aware of how strong you are.

So one particular day I wrote, 'I am Strong!' and what came up for me that day was:

- ⊙ I had the strength in yoga to maintain positions.

- ⊙ I stayed in the moment.

- ⊙ I was present.

- ⊙ I have a strong body.

- ⊙ I have an athletic body.

- ⊙ My mind is strong.

- ⊙ I maintain focus on each task I am working on.

- ⊙ I work diligently and work hard.

- ⊙ I love feeling strong because I can take on the world.

Now isn't that better than saying, 'I am not good enough', 'I am hopeless', 'I am useless' and so on? Could you imagine what the universe would come up with if you started your day off with that in your Evidence Journal instead?

We are not even going to go there!

Our first step is to create your Evidence Journal.

## STEP 2: YOUR STANDARDS

Your standards are how you expect yourself to operate on a daily basis. What you expect of you! You want to write out these standards and place them on the wall near your desk or in your bedroom, somewhere you can see them every day.

For example, some of my standards are:

⊙   I have respect for everyone I speak with.

⊙   I write in my Evidence Journal every day.

⊙   I wake up at five a.m. every morning.

⊙   I work out in the gym every day.

⊙   I eat a healthy breakfast, lunch and dinner that give me energy and focus.

⊙   I eat healthy snacks throughout the day to look after my body.

⊙   When I am working on my goals I am focused and stay present.

⊙   I set my intentions of what I want to achieve each day.

You get the point. But outline *your* new baseline standards of how you are going to operate on a daily basis.

Your second step is to create your Set of Standards.

## STEP 3: CONTROL OF YOUR EMOTiONS

Now this is a great exercise to do. You are going to work on controlling your emotions rather than have your emotions control you.

◎

Write down these questions in your journal:

1. What are the emotions that come up for you when you are told you are not good at something?

2. For each emotion, what comes up through the T.F.A.R (Thoughts, Feelings, Actions, Results) process?

3. How can you reframe each negative emotion through the T.F.A.R (Thoughts, Feelings, Actions, Results) process to give you a positive result?

One you have written out these questions it is time to get to work. Start identifying and figuring out how you can turn them around into a positive result instead of a negative one.

Write down and answer these questions below as well so you can identify the patterns that come up for you when you are told you are great at something:

1. What are the emotions that come up for you when are you told you are great at something?

2. For each emotion, what comes up through the T.F.A.R (Thoughts, Feelings, Actions, Results) process?

3. What have you noticed? What patterns are occurring for you?

Did you become more aware of how you are operating on an emotional level?

OK, so now you are becoming more and more aware, awesome!

**For the next 30 days, I want you to track your emotions**. Just write out in your journal when you are aware of your emotions. Don't judge them, just be aware of them and express what is going on for you in the moment and how you are feeling. It will enable you to identify how you are reacting or dealing with certain situations thrown at you.

As you become more aware you can then simultaneously work on your Emotional Standards.

## STEP 4: YOUR FOUR STEPS TO EMOTIONAL FREEDOM—EMOTIONAL STANDARDS

Here we are going to create your emotional standards. It's time to control those emotions. No more reacting, it's about staying in control. I am not saying here that you have to behave like a robot, it's perfectly fine to feel how you feel, but if you are feeling sad, down, frustrated, what are the action steps that are going to take place so you don't go down the path of your former habits?

When you notice an emotion that comes up, for example you feel sad, frustrated, angry or down, the first step you take is to acknowledge the emotion. It's OK to feel this way.

These four steps in sequence below are to help you understand how you can learn to control your emotions. It is about you taking control of yourself and not let your emotional reactions hold you back.

1.  Acknowledge the emotion. (*Just acknowledge you are feeling the emotion you are feeling*).

2.  Ask yourself; do I want to feel that emotion or do I want to change it?

3.  Ask yourself; what do I need to do to change that emotion immediately? (*This question is asking you how can you completely change it. It may be a physical movement, like jump around, or do some push ups, do a dance around, sing a song you love. You want to change that feeling instantly*).

4.  Ask yourself; what emotion can I replace it with to give me the ideal result I want?

Each time you notice your emotions getting out of control, take yourself back through these four steps to give you the more suitable result you ideally desire.

# CHAPTER 3

## LEARN THE SKiLLS

*'Through my education, I didn't just develop skills, I didn't just develop the ability to learn, but I developed confidence. – Michelle Obama*

Whatever it is that you will pursue in your life you will need to develop skills to succeed. These skills can be specific to your chosen sport, the skills of how to look after your body physically, the skills of how to build mental strength and toughness, the skills of how to communicate, the skills of how to control your emotions on and off the field for ultimate performance, the skills of how to get your body to perform at a nutritional level, the skills of how to build a business, the skills of how to deal with challenges and barriers… and so on.

You get my point!

Everything that you do will require you to learn and develop your skills. Tony Robbins constantly talks about mastery and mastering your skills. You MUST be constantly working on your skills and refining your skills to become the expert in every area of your life. The expert of YOU!

The best quote I have ever heard is: 'Every master was once a disaster' by David T.S. Wood.

This is true. We are a disaster when we start out. We know nothing about nothing, so how can we expect to know how to perform a skill or play a sport when we know nothing about it.

Golf taught me a lot about being a disaster. I went into learning golf thinking, 'How hard could this golf thing be? I am an accomplished tennis player and sportsperson.

Massive wake-up call! Golf taught me that it didn't matter how much skill I had in tennis or in any other sport I had played, I would have to start from the very beginning. You see, when you are an adult you expect that you should be able to do something instantly. Why can't I do this? I am an adult I, should be able to do this! However, when you are a child you understand that you must learn in order to improve. When starting something you haven't done before, you are not expected to know how to do it.

How can you know if you haven't done it before?

I have taught many kids tennis, golf and sports through the various businesses I have had. The kids get it. They know they are there to learn because they understand that they are young and that's the process. As long as they are learning skills in a fun way they keep coming back. The parents (adults) will encourage it because they want their kids to learn and they want their kids to have an enjoyable learning experience.

I have taught many adults tennis and, more recently over the past ten years, golf. Adults approach learning a new sport differently. They expect that they should be able to do it instantly. They expect that they should get the hang of 'this golf thing' within a couple of weeks. It places so much unwanted pressure on them. The pressure comes from within, from their expectation.

I have always said to clients who have come to work with me, on their golf especially, if they have just started out, 'This is going to take you three years to feel reasonably comfortable and to feel like you know what you are doing.' They all look at me with mouths hitting the floor, 'Three years? I don't have three years. I have to learn it now!'

The reason I say this is because it took me three years to feel comfortable about being on the golf course. It took me three years to have an understanding of the skills. It took me three years to perform better on the golf course in practice and under pressure in tournaments and competitions. And I was practising anything from four hours to twelve hours per day depending on whether I was working or whether I had the whole day off to work on my golf.

Yes, I went from a 45 to scratch handicap in three years, but I am not saying this to impress you, I am saying this to you to demonstrate that it will take time to develop your skills. It will take constant refinement so that you can become better and better.

When I started The Lady Golf Teacher business online, I had no clue. I didn't know what to do or how to start. I remember talking to a marketing expert and she asked, 'How do you market your business online?' I said, 'I'm a sportsperson and coach, I have no idea how to market online.'

That was a turning point. It was time to learn how to do that. I had to learn how to build my subscriber list, how to build my brand, how to build trust, how to market so that golfers would come and have golf lessons with me, buy my online programs and even join me on golf tours.

I knew nothing in this area. But, I didn't let that stop me. I knuckled down and learned everything I needed to know about building an online business, marketing, sales funnels and social media. Once I identified what worked and what didn't, I could then streamline it and simplify it so that it would work efficiently.

Again, do you know how long it took to learn those skills and feel comfortable? It took me about three years.

Tony Robbins always says at his events, 'People overestimate what they can do in a year and underestimate what they can do in a decade.' Yet in our current culture we live in an on-demand society. We expect everything to happen instantly. Why? Because we can pretty much get what we want by the push of a button. We can order virtually anything we want online and get it within twenty-four to forty-eight hours. Some services can do same-day delivery.

Yet, anything we want to achieve in our sport, our business, our life… it takes longer. It's frustrating, but it is a process. It is a process that you MUST work through and do, because if you don't you will never get want you want.

As I mentioned before, I have taught many adults golf. They want their skills to work yesterday. Sure, they will come and have lessons, sure they may participate in a weekly clinic; however, most don't go and work on their skills outside of that time, yet, they expect to improve!

Improvement and progression is slow for those who don't practice. They don't grasp the finer points that they need to refine, they just want the whole swing to work now. But it won't, not right now at the exact moment that they want it to, simply because they are not putting the time in outside of lesson time to practise.

Have you ever learned a musical instrument?

Learning an instrument is the same as learning a sport. It takes practice to learn the notes. It takes practice to learn how to play each note. It takes practice to string all the notes together to make it sound like lots of notes running into each other. it takes practice of lots of those notes running into each other to actually sound like music.

I have learned the guitar, and will constantly keep learning because it is such a pleasure to finally get those notes to sound like music. But I always compare learning the guitar to learning golf or anything in life.

Do you expect to be able to crank out a Beatles song, or any song, without ever picking up a guitar? Of course not, how could you? You don't know how to play.

So how could you do that with golf, or any sport you chose, or any business you chose to build or any big-ass dream that you are chasing. You have to start somewhere. We always start from the beginning, that's the best place to start.

The most important message I want you take away is that you MUST build foundations in anything that you do. Once you have the foundations in place it is easier. If the foundations are not built properly you will continue to struggle.

## FOUR STAGES TO LEARNING

### STAGE 1 – I DON'T KNOW WHAT I DON'T KNOW

In technical terms this is officially called Unconscious Incompetence. This doesn't refer to you being incompetent, it just means that you don't know what you don't know. Like the guitar, how can you play a song if you have never played a guitar before? It's not possible. So this just means that you don't know what to do because you haven't learned what to do.

### STAGE 2 – I AM BECOMING MORE AWARE BUT I STILL DON'T KNOW MUCH

In technical terms this is officially called Conscious Incompetence. Again, this stage doesn't refer to you being incompetent in a bad way, it just means that you are now more aware that there are skills you're required to learn and you are not that great at them, because you haven't learned them that well yet.

But you understand that you will need to learn them better in order to progress.

I find that most people will make a choice whether to continue through this stage and struggle with the learning or it is here that they will just give up, finding it way too hard. But, unfortunately for them, if they kept persisting they would realize that they *could* do it, it would just take work.

## STAGE 3 – I KNOW HOW TO DO THE SKILL BUT I HAVE TO CONCENTRATE

In technical terms this is officially called Conscious Competence. At this stage you are discovering that if you concentrate and focus on that skill at that moment in time you can accomplish that skill. But you are completely aware that you must focus when you are performing the skill because it does not happen automatically.

## STAGE 4 – CAN DO THIS SKILL IN AUTOMATIC MODE

In technical terms this is officially called Unconscious Competence. This means that you have learned and practised the skill so much that you have mastered it and you can do it in automatic mode. You don't have to think about it. You have practised it so much that it feels natural, it has turned into a habit.

# HOW LONG DOES IT TAKE TO LEARN A SKILL?

Everyone is an individual, therefore the amount of time to learn a skill will depend on the individual. There is no set length and it will depend on how much time you dedicate to learning the skill, receiving the proper coaching to learn the skill efficiently and effectively, and on how much time you give to practising and refining the skill.

Phillippa Lally, a health psychology researcher at University College London published a study in the *European Journal of Social Psychology*, she and her research team put together a study to figure out how long it actually takes to form a habit.

Over a twelve-week period, the study examined the habits of ninety-six people. Each person chose one new habit for the twelve weeks. Each day they then reported on that habit. They detailed whether or not they did the habit and how automatic the habit felt.

Some people chose simple habits like drinking a bottle of water with lunch. Others chose more difficult tasks like running for fifteen minutes before dinner. At the end of the twelve weeks, the researchers analysed the data to determine how long it took each person to go from starting a new habit to automatically doing it.

The result was, on average, about sixty-six days. But how long it takes a new habit to form can vary widely depending on the chosen habit, the person and the circumstances. In Lally's study, it took anywhere from eighteen days to 254 days for people to form a new habit.

Why do we need to understand that it can take a period of time to form a new habit or skill?

It tells us that we have to give ourselves time to learn and develop the skill, that how consistently we practise will affect how quickly we learn it, but that it will also depend on the complexity of the skill. That is, we can assume that a new habit such as drinking a bottle of water each day would be an easier habit to adopt than, for example, learning to play the guitar.

Therefore, learning the skill so that it becomes automatic will be conditional, not only on the complexity of the skill, but also on how much time is spent on learning the skill, being coached on the skill and refining the skill.

## HOW DO YOU BEST LEARN A SKILL?

We all learn skills in different ways. It is not one size fits all. We are all individual, therefore we have various ways in which we learn a skill. Learning a skill is easier once you understand how you learn and the ways that you are most receptive to information.

I remember being at school and the learning process that went on then. Most of it was telling you what to do. Some of it was writing it down from the chalkboard or overhead projector, copying into an exercise book and then what? We had to revise it!

That process of learning didn't work for me at all. Telling me what to do was an auditory way of teaching (I had to listen), and that just didn't work for me! I don't learn that way. Having me write something down, copy something, didn't work for me, as it didn't make sense to my preferred way of learning. But if something was explained practically—like being shown how to do something (visual), or where I could touch and feel it (kinaesthetic) and then repeat the same visual cues, it became much easier.

Therefore, sport for me was much easier to learn as the coach would show you, and then you would copy the movements, so you could feel it.

Because of this understanding that we all have various ways in which we learn a skill, I use three simple types of teaching. The visual (seeing), auditory (hearing) and kinaesthetic (feel and do). I will explain in more detail shortly.

When my niece Evelyn was nine years old, she had issues around learning maths at school. I found she would really open up when we walked together along the beach near her grandparents' (my parents house). So during a conversation with Evelyn, as we walked along the beach on a particular day, I asked her, 'Which way do you think is the best way that you learn?' She said, 'I need to be shown, I need to see what to do and then I need to feel how I do it through touching and doing.' She then went on to say, 'Yelling out numbers at me doesn't work, they get all muddled up in my brain.' Out of the mouth of a nine-year-old. Evelyn understood how *she* learned best.

## EiGHT TYPES OF LEARNiNG STYLES

Following are eight types of learning styles. You may find that you are a bit of each, but what I want you to identify is the *best way* in which you learn, because once you know how you learn then you can apply the strategies that work for you.

## THE LiNGUiSTiC LEARNER

The linguistic learner learns best through skills such as reading, writing, listening or speaking. For the linguistic learner to learn a new skill, their best method of learning would be to read about it, listen to a recording and take notes on it. To make the information concrete in their minds they would need to speak about it and write about it so that it is understood.

## THE NATURALiST

The naturalist learns skills through observation and experiences. They learn best through experimentation.

## THE MUSiCAL OR RHYTHMiC LEARNER

The musical or rhythmic learner uses melody and rhythm to learn. They learn through listening to music, rhythms or beats. It helps them through the learning process.

## THE KiNAESTHETiC LEARNER

The kinaesthetic learner learns a skill best by actually doing it. It's the hands-on experience that helps them learn because they can do, touch and feel the skill.

## THE ViSUAL OR SPATIAL LEARNER

The visual or spatial learner learns best through visual aids such as diagrams, pictures, graphs and video to enhance the learning experience. These learners tend to be more technical.

## THE LOGiCAL OR MATHEMATICAL LEARNER

The logical or mathematical learner learns best by classifying and categorizing. They tend to understand patterns, numbers and equations better than others.

## THE INTERPERSONAL LEARNER

The interpersonal learner learns best by relating to others. They share stories and compare their ideas to the ideas of others. By learning from and relating to others they are able to create new concepts and ideas.

## THE INTRAPERSONAL LEARNER

The intrapersonal learner learns best when they are alone. They are motivated internally and are not motivated or influenced by others around them.

Aren't the different ways in which you can learn interesting? Have you identified which learning style represents you best? What if you are a combination of some of them? The best way to approach this is to look at something you really love learning. What is your process when you learn?

I will give you an example. When I learn a skill, I have to be shown how to do it, but also have how to do it it explained to me whilst doing the actions. This means that my most important learning style is the Visual/Spatial Learner. I need to see it first. This is backed up by explanation telling me how to do it: which is the Linguistic Learner in me is now listening to how to do it. Then, as the Kinaesthetic Learner, I follow the visual and verbal instructions to perform the skill is being taught.

You can see that this occurs in a process. You are not just a learner who is categorized into just one learning area. You go through a process of steps to learn. What learning processes have you identified about yourself?

As you can see, there is not one way in which to learn, there are various methods. There is not a wrong style of learning, there is just a way in which you can learn best.

Once you know how you learn, then you apply that learning method to help you learn the skills you must have in order for you to achieve your goals and dreams in life.

# IS THERE A BEST WAY TO LEARN A SKiLL?

Is there a best way to learn a skill? In my experience of learning and teaching I feel that there is a process that you must take yourself through to learn a skill, so that you not only *can* learn it but you can *call* on it whenever needed in the future and it will still work for you.

The method I use is a Five-Step Process:

1. Chunk it down into individual pieces.

2. Slowly add each piece.

3. Make connections and transitions.

4. Go slow.

5. Find perfect rhythm.

# FiVE-STEP PROCESS TO LEARNiNG A SKiLL

## STEP 1: CHUNK iT DOWN iNTO iNDiViDUAL PiECES

I believe the best way to learn any skill is to chunk it down into individual pieces. You need to understand how each piece of the skill works. I learned this when I was at university doing my Human Movement degree. We had our biomechanics lecturer, Rob, teaching us how to play volleyball. I never was too fussed about volleyball, but what I learned about *how* we learned to play volleyball changed how I learned and taught everything from that point on.

What Rob did was break down each skill. We focused on three main skills: the pass, the set and the spike. I won't go through them in detail but what we did was learn the basic foundations for each skill. Once we could perform each basic skill we moved into building it up through progressions to the point where we were all playing a fully-fledged game with control and knowledge.

This is what I want you to understand: that whatever the skill you need to learn, you will need to break it down into separate pieces. Understand how each piece of the skill works.

I will explain it with a golf swing. There are seven major pieces to a golf swing.

⊙ Grip and setup

⊙ Takeaway

⊙ Top of swing

⊙ Down swing

⊙ Contact point

⊙ Follow through

⊙ Finish

So you can see here that we have separated the golf swing into seven separate pieces. What we then need to learn and work on is how to do each piece without having to connect them. We just learn each piece separately.

I won't go through them in major detail but it is the understanding of how each piece of the swing needs to be learned and practised, then how each piece will complement the next piece of the swing.

What about learning a song on the guitar? It may be a bit easier to see this broken down as there are fewer pieces.

We can break that down like this:

⊙ The chords of the song (could be three chords or more to learn)

⊙ The strumming or fingerpicking

What we need to do here is learn each chord separately to ensure we know how to play each chord, then learn the strumming or the fingerpicking technique required. We don't try to put it all together straight away, because we need to ensure that we can do each piece individually.

## STEP 2: SLOWLY ADD EACH PIECE

Now we have an understanding of the separate pieces of a skill, how do we add each piece together?

One piece at a time!

Where people struggle in learning skills is that they want all the pieces to work now and just get on with it. But what I want you to understand is that you need each piece of the skill to function well before you add each piece together. If you can't do each separate piece of the skill well, you will struggle to perform the skill.

Look at the starting point. What piece of the skill is the start?

Let's look at the golf swing again for the example. The starting point is the grip and the setup. This piece needs to be correct as it will complement every other piece of the swing that we add. So we make sure that piece is right. Then we connect the first piece to the second piece and see how they work together. For the swing it would be the grip and setup, then the takeaway. How do they work when they are connected? Do they connect well? Do they require more practice to ensure they are complementing each other, not hindering each other?

Once they work well together we then add another piece of the swing. I won't go through all the pieces but I want you to understand that we slowly add piece by piece back together so that each piece complements the other.

If we look at putting that song together with the guitar, we would start off with playing the first chord and strumming or fingerpicking that chord. Once we were fluent and comfortable with that we would then add the next piece, which is the next chord. So that once we have played the first chord, we then play the second chord and practise those two chords one after the other. Once they are working well together we add the third chord and so on. You get what I mean here.

Learning a skill is a progression of adding one piece at a time. Once one piece works you add on the next piece.

## STEP 3: MAKE CONNECTiONS AND TRANSiTiONS

What we want to do in this step is connect each piece together. In step 2 we were slowly adding each piece to see how each piece connected with the previous one. In this step we want all the pieces connected, so that we have an understanding of how each piece in the skill transitions to the next piece. Therefore we are still piecing together the skill, but in this step we are understanding how the pieces are connected and how to transition from one piece of the skill to the next.

For example, with our golf swing: we have the grip and setup. What is the transition for us to move into the takeaway position? Then how does the takeaway position transition to the top of the swing? And so on.

With the guitar, your transition will be changing from one chord to the next without losing the timing of the strum. It's about understanding how one chord flows on to the next chord.

## STEP 4: GO SLOW

Like learning to crawl before you can walk, you will need the skill to go slow before you speed it up. The reason you need to go slow, is that we may have connected all the pieces of the swing, we may have the transitions in place from one piece to the next, but we need to feel it in slow motion first. This is because we have to allow the development of the skill to take place in its time. If you rush this process you may then have to go back to step 3 or even step 2.

The purpose of this step is to feel the whole skill work together as one, but only slowly so that you can feel each piece working the right way and you can limit the amount of errors that will occur.

## STEP 5: FIND YOUR PERFECT RHYTHM

This is our final step in the process of learning a skill. Now that we can execute the skill in  slow motion and it feels good doing so, we can then up the rhythm. We can go faster and find that perfect flow.

We want to find that perfect flow of the skill so we will then be able to identify where we can perform that skill at its optimum. I call it finding that perfect rhythm, because it is finding the perfect rhythm for you: where you can perform the swing or the song with perfection.

Once you find your perfect rhythm that is where you stay and all you need to do is maintain it.

◎

Now let's work out the skills that you need to learn.

Get out your journal and answer these questions:

1. Which is the best way I learn?

2. What are the skills I must learn to help me achieve my dream?

3. How am I going to learn these skills? (Coaching, reading, video, etc.?)

4. For each skill, how will I apply the Five-Step Process For Learning A Skill?

5. When am I going to start working on these skills?

6. How much time will I allow to learn these skills?

7. Do I constantly work on refining these skills? (The answer to this one is *ABSOLUTELY!)*

# CHAPTER 4

# PRACTiCE, PRACTiCE, PRACTiCE (GRiNDiNG IT OUT)

*'Practice does not make perfect. Only perfect practice*
*makes perfect.'– Vince Lombardi*

Yes, that's right, you have to practise and then keep practising until it is perfect. There is another quote floating around that says 'practice makes perfect' but I prefer this one by Vince Lombardi NFL Coach: 'Practice does not make perfect. Only perfect practice makes perfect.'

We talked and discussed learning the skills you need in Chapter 3 and the process by which I suggest learning them, but now it's time to implement and practise these skills.

Remember I said in the last chapter that you have to get each piece of the skill right in order to transition into the next piece of the skill? Well, this is what we will be applying in this chapter. You are going to put in the time to learn and practise the skills you need so you can go out and get your dream to happen.

When I learned golf I was thirty-four years old. I knew nothing about the game, absolutely nothing. But I knew I had to learn the skills, I had to get a coach and then apply what I was learning. Some will say that the reason I progressed very quickly was because I was a natural sportswoman, but I believe it was because I understood the learning process and the practice process. I had not only come from another sport, tennis, that I was highly proficient at, but I had spent many years practising and training myself to pursue a professional sports career. I had also come from a teaching background, as I had taught tennis and had a sports-skills business to teach children sport, plus I had studied Human Movement at university.

Coming from playing a high level of tennis I knew that the only way to learn to play golf was to get on that range, the putting green, the chipping green and in the bunker and just grind it out over and over again, until I became proficient at the skills.

It was tough learning as an adult. I thought I would be able to do it much quicker because of my knowledge in training and my work ethic, but I still had to grind it out, I had to put the time and effort into practising.

Did I question what I was doing there?

Hell yeah!

I questioned myself all the time. It was tough, it was frustrating, I felt that no matter how many balls I was going to hit that day I just wouldn't get it. Especially in the beginning.

But I knew that if I just kept going, if I just kept practising the skills, getting on the course and putting those skills into action, grinding it out each day, that one day it would all come together.

Most people would have given up. I see it all the time through teaching golf. Most people don't really learn the skills properly and then they just won't give themselves the time to practise. They either give up or they complain that they can't get consistent. But the number-one reason they can't get consistent is that they just don't practise enough, and if they do practise, they don't practise what they need to practise.

This is why I did so well in a short period of time compared to most golfers, because I focused on getting the skills to be mechanically efficient and I practised them over and over to get them consistent, so that I could perform them whenever I needed to.

That is the difference between someone who wants to achieve and someone who wants to dabble. I am not knocking the person who wants to dabble, but it is like you are just putting your toe in the water and that's about all the commitment you will give it, just a bit.

If you really want to achieve your dream, you have to go all in, give it all you have got, practise, practise and practise until you can do it with your eyes closed, so that you can do it on autopilot. That's what it will take.

The difference between those who are successful and those who are not, is that those who are successful do the work, they put in the hard yards, the practice and they grind it out. Those who are not successful just walk away and say it was all too hard. They give up.

Grinding it out is all part of getting your skills in place for taking the next step to achieve your dream.

◎

Michelangelo, Renaissance sculptor and painter who spent four years lying on his back to paint the ceiling of the Sistine Chapel said, 'If people knew how hard I had to work to gain my mastery, it wouldn't seem wonderful at all.'

Michelangelo worked away at his craft daily. It was the actions, the strokes, refining his technique daily that enabled him to be able to create the artwork he produced.

It's that 'talent versus hard work' theory or the 'born versus made' debate. You see an athlete perform and think, 'Wow what a talent.' But what a lot of people neglect to understand is all the hard work, the practice, the grind that goes on behind the scenes for it to look so natural.

Michael Jordan, legendary basketballer, spoke with a group of journalists about how it had bothered him that people tended to think of him as a natural-born athlete. What concerned Jordan was the underestimation of all the hard work he had done to become that legendary athlete. Jordan has this awesome video that will explain what grinding it out is. It is called 'Maybe It's My Fault'.

He says in this video:

*Maybe it's my fault.*

*Maybe I led you to believe, it was easy when it wasn't.*

*Maybe I made you think my highlights started at the free-throw line and not in the gym.*

*Maybe I made you think that every shot I took was a game winner, that my game was built on flash and not fire.*

*Maybe it's my fault that you didn't see failure as strength, my pain was my motivation.*

*Maybe I led you to believe that basketball was a god-given gift and not something I worked for every single day of my life.*

*Maybe I destroyed the game or,*

*Maybe you are just making excuses.*

Those words get me deep into my core and bring tears to my eyes. Because that's what it is all about. In order to have the glory there is a story, you have got to put the hard work in, you have got to do the practice and you have got to grind it out.

*You may be thinking, 'Tiff, this sounds hard!' But this is REALITY!*

You MUST do the WORK!

You MUST make the EFFORT!

Yes, it will be TOUGH!

If you want it—you have got to GRIND IT OUT!

## HOW MUCH TIME TO DEDICATE TO PRACTISING?

I am going to give you a simple answer to this one. As much time as you can dedicate!

Remember you are learning the skills and you are practising these skills until you can do it in automatic mode. How long it takes to make these skills automatic will depend on you.

- ⊙ It will depend on how much time you dedicate to practising.

- ⊙ It will depend on how you are learning each piece of the skill.

- ⊙ It will depend on how receptive you are in learning each piece of the skill.

- ⊙ It will depend on how patient you are in piecing together the skill.

- ⊙ It will depend on how you can get the skill to flow.

So my advice here is to dedicate and refine the skill as much as you can, to the point where you don't have to think about it, it will just happen.

For Serena Williams, one of the greatest tennis player's of all time, did just that when she was growing up and learning tennis. She went with her dad (her coach) and her sister Venus, and they practised and refined their foundational skills for years. They did it daily, before and after school, and all weekend. They both got their skills so refined, so perfected, that when it came time to perform they didn't have to think about how the skill worked, they could just do it. It was automatic: they just moved to the ball wherever the ball needed to be directed. But this came from years of practice and dedication.

*How much time will you spend practising your skills so that they become automatic and feel natural?*

## PRESSURE PRACTiCE

Not only will you have to dedicate time to practice, once the skill is learned you will then have to apply pressure to learning the skill, so that you can perform under pressure.

How important is pressure practice?

It is everything. You can practise as much as you like, you can grind it out as much as you like, but at the end of the day, if you can't perform your skills under pressure, you will struggle.

Struggle may even be the thing that causes you to give up. I see it with golfers that I have taught over the years and players I have watched. They just can't cope under pressure. It's not necessarily the pressure of a competition, it can even be the pressure that comes from within. It all gets too much, they get too anxious, they crumble and they give up.

This is what happened to me playing that tournament tennis match against the Australian ranked professional. I had placed so much pressure on myself to perform that I got overwhelmed and crumbled. That pressure was not from her, but from within me.

I didn't know how to deal with pressure, I didn't know how to cope with my emotions under pressure and I completely broke down. The simple reason was that I hadn't prepared myself under pressure. Sure, I had many practice matches with peers at the tennis academy but the problem wasn't being resolved in those matches. In practice matches I hadn't learned the strategies to help deal with practising under pressure, therefore I couldn't perform when it came to competing in tournaments.

My niece, Evelyn, when she was eleven years old, had a try out for the dance team at school in jive, cha-cha and the tango. She loves to dance, that's her thing. She dances around the house, practising the steps every time someone puts music on. Yet when she was at school and it was trial time to get into the team, she said, 'Aunty Tiff, my mind went blank and I forgot all the steps.'

How could that happen you ask? Wasn't Evelyn practising? Of course she was, she looks like a natural to me (it's her gift, and yes I am biased) but she hadn't practised under pressure. She hadn't put herself in a situation of practising under pressure, in order to know how she could cope with the pressure she would put upon herself. Given that she was only eleven years old, of course she can, and will need to, *learn* how to cope with pressure.

You can only practice to a certain point for refinement because to conquer and perform in tournaments or an event, a speech, whatever it may be, you will need to have strategies in place that will help you progress. Otherwise you will be held back in your development and you may even quit!

## HOW TO PRACTISE UNDER PRESSURE

You can apply this methodology in any area, not only sport, because in life we will encounter times when we feel under pressure. It's how we deal with the pressure that will be the key to our successes.

I am going to assume that at this point, when you begin to practise under pressure, that you have refined your skills so that you have confidence in them, and that you can perform the skills on demand, when you require them.

The essence of practising under pressure is for you to mimic a pressure situation that will occur during a tournament, or some type of event, so that you are prepared for it and will then know how to deal with it at the key time.

## MiMiC PRESSURE SiTUATiONS

The key to successful practice under pressure is to mimic situations that you will encounter. Therefore it is essential that we establish what you must do here.

Time to get out your journal and start working on this now.

### SEVEN STEPS TO DEALiNG WiTH PRESSURE SiTUATiONS

1.  Think of a situation that comes up for you—a situation that really makes you feel anxious, where you go into a panic and you feel under pressure every time you encounter it.

    ⊙ How does it make you feel?

    ⊙ What emotions come up for you?

    ⊙ What do you start thinking?

    ⊙ What do you say to yourself?

    ⊙ What type of language do you use? Do you swear at yourself, are you mean and angry towards yourself, or are you nice to yourself?

    ⊙ Are you worried about looking like an idiot or embarrassing yourself?

    ⊙ How does your body feel? Does your body freeze and tighten up? Do

you get sweaty palms? Does your heart feel as though it is going to burst out of your chest because it is beating so fast?

⊙   Do you notice anything else that comes up for you?

2.   Now that you are aware of what is going on for you in this situation, how would you like to handle this situation in the future? The way you are now handling it and continuing down the same path? Or would you like to change it and deal with it so you can push through that barrier? (I am going to assume you have said, 'Tiff, I would love to change it because it is not serving me to be this way, as I feel like I am stopping myself from pushing forward!')

3.   Explain in detail the way in which you want to handle this situation.

⊙   How are you going to feel?

⊙   What type of emotions do you want to come up for you to deal with in this situation?

⊙   What do you want to think?

⊙   What do you want to say to yourself?

⊙   What type of language do you want to use in this moment: affirmations, trust, calming?

⊙   What are the words you want to say in this moment?

⊙   Are you displaying confidence and standing tall?

⊙   How do you want your body to feel?

- ⊙ Do you want your body to feel relaxed?

- ⊙ Do you want your heart to be calm or beating fast to keep you alert?

- ⊙ Anything else that you want to do or be in this situation?

4. How are you going to mimic this situation in practice?

    - ⊙ How are you going to set up this situation in practice so that you can practise how you are going to handle it?

5. How often are you going to visualize this situation and how are you going to respond?

6. What is the preparation process that you are going to take yourself through before you go out there to compete or perform whatever the event or task may be? How are you going to mentally prepare yourself on game day?

    - ⊙ Will you visualize?

    - ⊙ Will you go through a breathing technique?

    - ⊙ Will you psych yourself up? How?

    - ⊙ What else will you need to do?

7. Game On—Now Just Go and Do!

    - ⊙ After you have performed, just be aware of how you have handled the situation. We will be spending a chapter on feedback, but for this right now just be aware of how you responded when this situation came up for you.

    - ⊙ Did you respond better?

⊙   Or do you need to spend more time on refining it?

OK, this is great, you now have a strategy in place for how to deal with pressure in a situation that comes up for you.

Now what you want to do is identify all the pressure situations that come up for you and repeat the seven-step process for each and every one of them.

It's time to deal with the pressure now so don't avoid it. Take it head on, because you will encounter this with everything that you do in your life. The time to deal with it is now. Dealing with it now will give you the confidence to take on any pressure situation, this in turn will teach you to grow and move forward, not to be held back by pressure, but to embrace it and get on with it!

## CHAPTER 5

# LEARNiNG FROM MiSTAKES
# (DON'T BE FRiGHTENED TO MAKE THEM)

*'Life is all about evolution. What looks like a mistake to others has been a milestone in my life. Even if people have betrayed me, even if my heart was broken, even if people misunderstood or judged me, I have learned from these incidents. We are human and we make mistakes, but learning from them is what makes the difference.'* – Amisha Patel

You may hear this from many personal-development leaders, business leaders, teachers, parents and, yes, even me, but it is learning from your mistakes that will be the thing that will catapult you forward.

People are frightened of making mistakes because they see or have interpreted that they themselves have failed. And when you have failed a number of times you are frightened of failing again. You then develop this belief that you fear failure, and because you then fear failure you are too frightened to take action. Then, when you are too frightened to take action, you just settle. You then will get angry with yourself, not trust yourself, not trust anyone, be constantly frustrated within and with those around you. You will be disappointed that you have let yourself down, you'll say the most negative words to yourself, beat yourself up and put yourself down. From that, you will attract the wrong people into your life and allow them to treat you badly because you think you deserve it. You will live life with constant regret and because you will feel so miserable, your health will deteriorate, you will have no energy, you will simply go through the motions, your life will become dull and you will be dull. All of this because at some point in your life you were frightened of making a mistake.

You might be thinking, 'Hey, Tiff, that is really intense!' But, I will tell you that this is true and it happens over and over again. Because if you are frightened of making mistakes and you feel it often enough, you will be constantly frightened of making mistakes and this will hold you back. Then you will get the snowball effect that was mentioned in the above paragraph.

Earlier in this book I shared with you a personal-development program that I attended where it was explained that at certain ages in our lives, we make decisions about the world. Well these decisions can include developing a fear of failure, a fear of making a mistake.

When I was ten years old I was playing a tennis tournament, one of my first tournaments. It was exciting and nerve wracking at the same time, but I loved just being on the court. It was my world, my everything!

In this tournament, I was playing against another ten-year-old girl, who was from the city. This girl was supposed to be the best player in our age group in the state. Anyway, I absolutely smashed this girl in the first set 6–0. It was amazing. I was doing everything right, hitting the ball exactly where I wanted it to go, whereas she struggled. I felt on top of the world.

Then, something went snap in my brain. I thought, 'What if I lose? What if I put in all this effort and I lose the game? I would be a failure!' Guess what happened? I lost the match. I lost the next two sets convincingly. I can't remember the score, it is a blur to me, but I remember that moment of fear and I realized it was what defined me from that point forward. That moment told me that if I worked hard and gave everything I had and I still lost, I would be a failure.

Isn't it amazing that at ten years old we can think that way? I look back now and think, 'Tiff, you missed so many awesome opportunities, you didn't get to pursue your dream of being the number-one tennis player in the world, simply because you were frightened of making a mistake!'

Wow! That's intense!

But it is true. I spent the rest of my tennis life still wanting to be that tennis professional I had always dreamed about, but there was always something that was holding me back. I was frightened of making mistakes, I was frightened of putting all the effort in and still losing. It became all-consuming. Yet, even though this was what I was feeling deep down (not that I was aware of it), I still managed to win tournaments and matches, but most players who were better mentally prepared than I was beat me the majority of the time because they were not afraid of making mistakes.

Imagine living life that way.

I did until I was thirty-five years old.

I feared making mistakes and I feared that I was never good enough in anything that I did. And because of that fear of failure, the fear of making mistakes, they way I felt about myself was affected. I thought I was nothing. I thought I had no importance in the world. I even attracted the wrong men into my life because of how I felt within: a failure. I allowed them to control me.

Even though this was how I felt within I still managed to get a university degree. I still started two businesses that ended up being very successful. How was this possible if I feared failure? It was because I didn't personally attach myself to the businesses. I saw them as businesses in which I could help and make a difference to kids' lives. The kids were learning sports skills in one business, then I would move them when they were ready into the tennis-coaching business. I was teaching the kids sports skills, teaching them to trust their abilities, teaching them how to work as a team and socialize with other players in their group. It was wonderful. Again, this was successful because it wasn't about me, it was about showing the kids how to be confident within, how to trust their judgements and have a great time learning.

The turning point came when I was thirty-five years old. I started reading books on developing myself into the person I wanted to become: I attended personal-development programs, I started working on me. I did this because at that one particular personal-development course I realized I was holding myself back because I believed that I wasn't good enough. I was now aware that it was me who held myself back, it was me who believed I wasn't good enough, it was me who feared failure, it wasn't anyone else. It was me, it was my responsibility that I believed I was this way.

I started working on me because I had discovered my next big love. I had discovered golf and I felt the same about it as I had felt about tennis growing up. It was my everything, and I saw it as my chance to still go down the path of being a professional athlete.

There was a snag though. I realized I was behaving the same way I did all those years ago with tennis. My demons were coming back to haunt me. I was frightened of making mistakes. I was frightened of failing. I was putting myself down all the time, telling myself that I was having myself on. I quite often said, 'Tiff, this is too hard, you are a joke, who do you think you are that you could play golf and even become a professional!'

Sounds familiar doesn't it?

Tennis days revisited.

I sought out help with various sports psychologists, constantly read personal development books and attended courses in an effort to not let this happen again: to not let this fear of making mistakes, this fear of failure, hold me back from moving forward to achieve my next important dream.

One day when I was playing a golf tournament, again, something went snap in my brain. But it was a good snap, not like the tennis snap when I was ten. I said to myself, 'Tiff, you keep making these same mistakes with your golf swing over and over because you are not trusting yourself. What if you let that lack of trust go? Focus and stay in the moment and give it your best chance. How do you think that will go?' I said to myself, 'Yes, Tiff, that's right. It is not working the other way so let's just do the best you can in that moment and if it doesn't work you'll get feedback on why it didn't work.'

Could you imagine what it then did to my golf game? This was why I was able to get to a scratch handicap in three years. This was why I started teaching golf after four years of learning to play, because I changed my approach from fearing mistakes and fearing failure, to using mistakes and errors as feedback and learning from them.

## IT IS OK TO MAKE MiSTAKES

This was why I shared my story with you: my tennis experiences and the feelings around mistakes and failures. And then having the realization when I was playing a golf tournament that it's OK to make mistakes because mistakes are just feedback.

Whether we do something well or we do something not so well, and it either works or doesn't work, it is just feedback.

I have taught so many women over sixty who want to learn to play golf. But this fear of making a mistake, the fear of failure, the fear of looking like an idiot, holds them back from progressing. Why?

Because they too fear that mistakes and errors are bad. They don't trust their decisions, they don't trust their judgement. Where do you think all of that stems from? Yes, that's right, they made decisions growing up that mistakes are bad (some of it we learned at school: you know when you see that big red X next to an answer). So it takes constant work of building them up to look at each error that occurs as just being feedback.

Mistakes don't mean what you have done is wrong, they just mean that what you did didn't work in that moment and there was a reason that it didn't work. You just need to figure out what that reason was, why there was an error or mistake and learn from that feedback.

## HAVE YOU EVER MADE A MiSTAKE?

Of course you have made a mistake. We all make mistakes. We make decisions about whether we will do something, then we do that one thing and we get a result. Sometimes that decision may have not been the best decision then, hey presto, a mistake or error happens.

But do you know what is so good about that?

We won't do it again, will we? If we were paying attention we won't make it again, but if we weren't paying attention then it is possible we will.

Lots of mistakes tend to happen when we are kids because we haven't had as many experiences as adults yet, simply because we haven't been around long enough. When I was ten years old (there seem to be a few things that happened when I was ten—lots of turning points, anyway, back to the story), it was pouring with rain and my Mum was taking us over to Dad's work. We had to jump out of the car and run down a hill towards a verandah so we wouldn't get too wet.

I thought, 'Great, I am going to race my sister down the hill in the pouring rain and beat her there.' We both jumped out of the car, I pushed her out of the way so I could win (my competitive nature), then I slipped on the footpath and broke my arm. Serves me right anyway, for pushing my sister out of the way.

The mistake was running in an unsafe environment: the pouring rain. What I learned after having my arm in a cast for six weeks was that I never wanted to be in a cast again. It stopped me from playing tennis, climbing trees, pushing a billy cart around town and more for the next six weeks. Thus the lesson learned was a painful and restrictive one, and I didn't want to experience the result again.

But can you imagine if I hadn't paid attention to that lesson? It could have *definitely* happened again.

You can see this is how we learn.

If we climb a tree and fall out, then next time we climb the tree, we don't put our foot in the spot that caused us to fall. We figure out a better spot on the branch to place our foot so we don't fall out of the tree again.

It is all trial and error. In order for us to learn, we have to experience something. We try it out and then we see whether it works or whether it doesn't. It definitely doesn't mean that we don't try the experience again, it just means we try it a different way.

Look at relationships. If you have a bad experience with a person that you got involved with, it doesn't mean that you shouldn't be in a relationship with anyone again, even though that's definitely how you feel at the time—'Never ever going to get involved with anyone ever again!'

But, the most important thing is that you learn from that relationship. If it was a bad experience (a mistake), what did you learn?

The reason I bring this up is because life is all trial and error. We don't really know what something is like until we experience it. If we go out on a date with someone, we find, hey, that person is OK. Then we get involved in a relationship with them and discover there is something that is not right. They make us feel bad about ourselves or that we are not good enough in their eyes, or that whatever we do is not right. There will be a feeling that will come up for you, telling you that something is not right. Listen to that feeling or those feelings. You are being taught a lesson.

The question is whether or not you are going to listen to those lessons. It took me a while to listen to those lessons being taught. I got involved with a few men along the way for all the wrong reasons. For me it was because I felt so poorly about mysel. I thought I was a nothing and a failure in life, at the ripe old age of twenty-five (thinking I was Miss Experience). I tended to put up with these men because I didn't believe I was good enough for anything better. It was OK that they spoke to me poorly, stood me up on dates, flirted with other women and treated me like an idiot because I didn't think I was anything flash. I thought I was ugly and I didn't think I deserved any better. I used to tell myself constantly what a failure I was in life, so I just put up with it.

Could you imagine living life this way? It scares me to think I was ever in that place in my mind. But I was. I was trying to figure out my place in the world because I didn't achieve my dream and to me, that meant I was a failure.

Luckily I listened. It took me a while but I did listen. I listened to a few people around me. One was a close friend and tennis client. She insisted I seek out help. I did listen because I could no longer go through the tears each day. I would cry as soon as I woke up, I would cry all my way to work. I would then work quite well because it took my mind off things. But then I would drive home, crying all the way, cry myself to sleep and repeat it all again the next day. What an awesome life. Not!

I got to the point where I just couldn't live my life like that anymore. I never ever felt suicidal, but I just knew I couldn't deal with living life like this. I wasn't meant to live my life that way and no one should ever live their life that way.

When I was at an appointment speaking with a psychologist, she said, 'Tiff, I have seen women put up with this for decades, do you want this to be you?' I said, 'No!' I continued to cry my eyes out for the rest of the session.

But from that point on, I made changes. I really started looking at what the problem was. What were the mistakes I was making? I was blaming the men I was attracting. They were all the same, controlling and mean, but it wasn't them. It was me!

Of course, they were controlling and so on, but it was me that had the problem because I allowed them to treat me that way. It was time to work on me!

What was the lesson learned here?

The lesson i learned was that my very poor opinion of myself, and my feeling that I was a big failure in life, affected every single decision I made. That was a big mistake, wasn't it? Thinking I was a failure. Because up until that point, I had the chance to play professional tennis overseas, I had a university degree, I had two successful businesses, had begun to play golf and was working towards a golf career.

## WHAT ABOUT YOU?

As you can see, we all make mistakes. We make poor choices. We are not perfect (as much as we would like to be), but we have experiences in life, on the court, and on the field. The key is how we deal with them and how we learn from them.

Does my  sharing these stories with you, make you think about mistakes you have made in your life?

Grab your journal. Let's take a look at some of them right now. Get them out in the open.

1.  List mistakes that really stand out for you.

2.  For each mistake, what do you believe caused that mistake? Why did that mistake happen?

3.  For each mistake, did you repeat that mistake over and over?

4.  If yes, why?

5.  If no, what did you learn from each of those mistakes?

6.  Is there a new way that you can approach a mistake when it happens in the future?

How did you feel after doing this exercise? If you felt that this brought up a lot about you making mistakes and weird feelings about them then this is great. That's because we want to we want to reposition your mind about how you think and feel about mistakes.

Remember, it is truly OK that we make mistakes and errors in judgement. The most important thing is that we learn from them and we grow from them. They won't be what define us, they will be what develop us into amazing human beings so that we can take on any challenge and move us in the direction that we want to go.

*Mistakes = Feedback.*

OK, so now we understand that it is alright to make mistakes. This is how we are going to learn and grow from them. They are just experiences that teach us lessons; they give us feedback on how to improve.

This is what we are going to work on now: not to let mistakes hold us back, but to let mistakes enable us to be what we want to be and to do what we want in our lives.

*Event + Response = Feedback.*

Look at the equation above. An event happens to which we respond, then we achieve an outcome (feedback).

Let's look at passing a tennis player at the net.

There is your opponent at the net, your opponent has returned the ball back over the net to the forehand court, you move across to your forehand side to hit the ball, to pass your opponent down the line, but the ball hits the net.

So we have:

*Event = The ball has come to your forehand side.*

*Response = You attempt to pass your opponent.*

*Feedback = Your ball hits the net.*

Now is that a mistake? No, it's just feedback, isn't it? It just shows that you wanted to pass your opponent down the line but it didn't happen because the ball hit the net.

When that happens again do you think, 'Oh well, that didn't happen last time so I should just give up and not try because it will just happen again.'? Or do you think, 'OK, I am going to try it again but this time I have to make sure I clear the net, or maybe I should pass my opponent cross court or even lob over their head.'?

I know you are saying, 'Tiff, I am going to try it a different way this time!' That's great, that's the way you must be thinking.

It is trial and error. You have to keep experimenting to see what works, and you just keep repeating it over and over until it does work. If it doesn't work, try something else and keep testing, trialling and tweaking.

It is really interesting watching my six-year-old niece, Lillian, grow up. She has an incredible approach to learning. She never wants your help to do anything. From the moment she was able to walk, she would say, 'I do myself.' Now she is six and she won't have it that you help her with anything, she wants to figure it out on her own. I applaud her tenacity, she is trying to figure out how to do things herself. She will observe you (not let you show her, but will watch you when you are not looking), then she will keep trialling and changing it about until she gets it. She can come across as being stubborn (and she can be challenging at times) but she is determined that through trial and error she can figure it out.

⊙

Get out your journal and write down this simple equation:

*Event + Response = Feedback.*

Let's take a look at a prominent event that is occurring in your life right now that is not working. It could be something in your sport, your life or your business.

⊙   Write it out: What is not working?

⊙   What is the event?

⊙   What is your current response?

⊙   What is the feedback you are receiving about it?

Now I want you to brainstorm how we can fix it so you get the feedback you desire from it.

We are going to work backwards to create it.

1.   What is the feedback you ideally want to receive from this current event?

2.   What is the type of response you want to have from this current event?

3.   What is the current event?

All we have done here is reframe it. The new equation is:

*Feedback + Response = Event.*

You see, if we work backwards we can figure out what we ideally want to achieve and then figure out the steps to make it happen.

Now look at everything that is going on in your life, every aspect. Look at everything that you want to improve.

How can you use this formula to make events that are occurring in your life better? Look at:

- ⊙ what you are eating,

- ⊙ your fitness,

- ⊙ the relationships in your life,

- ⊙ your sport performance,

- ⊙ how you communicate with people,

- ⊙ your business, your work or school,

- ⊙ your values,

- ⊙ your standards,

- ⊙ and much more… the above list is simply to trigger you

As you can see, you can reframe everything that is occurring in your life that you see as mistakes, as FEEDBACK. Then you can study the feedback to work out what you need to do to improve things in your life.

# CHAPTER 6

# THE OBSTACLES YOU WiLL FACE

*'All the adversity I've had in my life, all my troubles and obstacles, have strengthened me... You may not realize it when it happens, but a kick in the teeth may be the best thing in the world for you.' – Walt Disney*

You will always encounter obstacles. They will always be in your way, challenging you and testing you. The reason this happens is, as I always say, the universe is testing you to see how badly you want to achieve this dream.

Look at it this way: you have worked out what your dream is, you know what you want to do and what you want to achieve. Then you get started on achieving your dream; it is exciting and it is fun, you know what you want, but then all of a sudden, 'Bam!'

You are at a standstill. The dream you want begins to be hard, you seem to be working your butt off and can't see any progress. It becomes boring because you are now doing the same thing day in and day out. You start to question yourself. You ask the question, 'Will I ever make it? It seems like I am so far away, I don't know if I will ever get there.'

You most likely will be thinking, 'I didn't think this was so hard. How come others make it look so easy, it is really tough for me, am I doing this the right way? Is there an easier way? Why is this so hard for me? Why can't I be like everyone else and just go through the motions?'

I will tell you why you are feeling this way: it's because you are an achiever. You want more from your life and you want more from you. You don't believe that you were born and brought to this earth just to go through the motions, you are here for a reason. You are here to have an impact in this world. You are here to have *your* impact!

There is no possible way you can just go through the motions. It is not possible for you. Perhaps for others it is OK to just go through the motions but not for you!

You know what? Your dream is tough. It is going to be hard work. You are going to be challenged. You are going to have obstacles in your way. There will be brick walls. Whether you want to hear this or not, this is reality and it is all part of the process.

Look at all the people that you greatly admire. You so badly want to be like them, you see the glory of what they have achieved. They could be a world-class athlete raking in all the sponsorship endorsements and winning tournaments. You look at them and say, 'Yeah, I want to be like them!' Or perhaps you see an entrepreneur or an actor who has their private jet, flying around the world giving interviews, living a lavish lifestyle and you say, 'Yeah, I want to be like them!'

Whoever it is that you admire, you see that person where they are at now in their career. You haven't seen behind the scenes, the arduous work they have put themselves through. You only see the glory, you haven't heard the story of how they got there.

I want you to be aware that there will be challenges ahead because this is normal. I also want to share with you right now, before you hear some great stories about working through the obstacles, what happens if you choose not to work through the challenges you will face.

As you have read through these chapters I have pointed out to you many times that I wanted to be the number-one tennis player in the world. You are also aware that that dream didn't happen. Why?

I hit so many obstacles and I didn't know how to work through them. I didn't have the guidance. I had the support of my parents, but they didn't know how to help me. I so badly wanted to play tennis, it was my everything, but I didn't know what to do.

I trained at a tennis academy after I finished school but I didn't know I was encountering obstacles, I thought I just wasn't good enough. It wasn't that at all. It wasn't that I didn't work hard because I worked my butt off for ten hours a day. It was that I didn't know how to work through everything that was thrown my way.

Here are some obstacles I encountered:

1. I hit flat forehands not top spin.

2. I had slice backhand no top-spin backhand.

3. I worked hard in training but lost tournament matches.

4. I worked harder and harder but I wasn't improving.

5. I had no belief in me so was down on myself all the time.

6. I was doing the same thing over and over expecting a better result.

Instead of asking the coaches questions and saying, 'How come I hit my balls differently to everyone else, is there something I need to know?' Or, 'Why am I losing matches all the time, what do I need to do, what do I need to work on?' I would just work harder on what I had. I was shy and never spoke up. Do I blame the coaches? No, I don't, because I really don't think they knew what they were doing either.

When I played tennis overseas, I was losing matches in every tournament. But I never asked myself this one simple question, 'What is it that I need to do to win matches?' If I had only known that one simple thing to do was to ask myself, 'How can I get better?' If I had known that I could be resourceful and figure it out, then I could have been writing a very different book.

Don't live life with regret and wish that you had given everything you had. Don't give up because it has been tough lately. It's tough for all of us. We all go through it. I am here to share with you what I have learned along my sport and life journey; to show you some hacks and lessons and to show you how to get there quicker than I did. Even though I didn't achieve my first dream as a kid, watch this space because there is a big dream in the making as I write this book that I will share later. But right at this moment, I want you to take note that you *will* encounter some obstacles and that you *will* have to work through them.

## THE MOST MAGiCAL PLACE ON EARTH HAD OBSTACLES?

Have you ever visited Disneyland, 'the most magical place on earth'?

Walt Disney, an entrepreneur, cartoonist, film producer and creator of the world's best-known theme park, encountered many obstacles when he had the vision of creating Disneyland.

Everyone Walt Disney approached about building Disneyland knocked him back. Bankers, investors and many people within his company opposed the idea of building a theme park. His brother Roy thought that a 'fanciful, expensive amusement park would lead to financial ruin'.

Walt was confident of his vision (he had a big-ass dream) and started to accumulate the finance required to fund the team that could make his dream come true. He sold vacant land and borrowed against his life insurance. He hired a team of people to start the design and layout of the park. But he still didn't have the location nor the funds to create his dream.

Disney hired the Stanford Research Institute to examine the economic prospects of developing Disneyland and to scout a Southern California location. A suitable location was found. But in order to secure funding for the construction of Disneyland, Walt had to begin pitching to gain the finance for the creation of the theme park.

Two television networks declined his proposed deal with them and the theme park, but through the help of his brother and an artist friend who drew a detailed map of the future Disneyland, he approached another television network. Walt agreed with the network to run a television series and the funding for his dream of Disneyland had begun.

Walt Disney had a dream and a vision, but he hit obstacles everywhere he turned. Many people didn't share his dream, nor would they back it financially. Therefore he himself worked through solving the problems he encountered. He didn't let anything hold him back and he found a way to make his vision of Disneyland a reality.

Walt was clever, a real marketer ahead of his time. He used his television series to promote his vision of Disneyland. He would show the detailed map of his theme park - his plan of what they were building - creating hype and sharing stories of the construction and of where they were at with the development. He took his viewers on the journey with him, from the drawing - his original vision - to turning it into a reality: a real live theme park where you could be a big kid for a day and have the time of your life.

There were close to 15,000 people invited for Disneyland's opening day in 1955, however there had been counterfeit tickets issued and around 28,000 people showed up. Many challenges were faced on opening day. It was hot, there were problems right throughout the park plus an extra 13,000 people to deal with. Many reports consider that opening day was a disaster, and yet Disneyland still became the success it is today (and has been for decades).

What did Walt do when he hit an obstacle?

He would go to work to find a solution. He didn't know anything about construction and development, so he sought out experts in those fields and hired them to develop a construction timetable for his dream. He found experts to examine the economic prospects of Disneyland and scout the perfect location for the theme park. He couldn't fund the project himself, therefore he set up a deal to produc a television series to finance his venture.

At times you are going to feel like you are hitting brick walls. Don't let the barriers be the devices that stop you from achieving. If you hit a barrier then you want to always be looking for ways to solve the problem that you have encountered.

The reality is that you will always come across barriers, obstacles, challenges and brick walls but it is how you work through them that is the key. Building success is not just about learning the skills and doing the skills, it is also about seeking expert guidance, believing in your vision and getting to work to make it happen.

Look at Walt Disney: he had certain skills in some areas, and where he didn't, he would either learn the skills or work with experts to assist him to achieve his vision. He encountered many barriers but he was open to new possibilities and was mentally determined to achieve his dream. Walt did everything he could possibly do to make his theme park turn into 'the happiest place on earth'.

## PUSHiNG THROUGH THE BARRiERS

You have got to push through the barriers. It is going to be so hard. I say that it will be hard because we live in a society today that tries to make everything easy. We have so much technology to help us do this, that and the other, yet when it comes to achieving the ultimate dream it is going to take effort, it is going to take work, it is going to take time, it is going to take courage and it is going to take mental strength. It is going to take everything you have got. You are going to have to do the work, that is true and that is the reality.

◎

Let's do a quick exercise right now before we continue.

Write down in your journal: *What Are the Top 3 Times I Have Hit A Wall?*

1. .......................................................................... ?

2. .......................................................................... ?

3. .......................................................................... ?

For each time when you hit a wall, following are some questions for you to consider to explain in as much detail as you can what you went through when you hit a wall.

⊙ Where were you?

⊙ Who were you with?

⊙ Were you alone?

⊙ How old were you?

⊙ What year was it?

⊙ What happened to cause you to hit a wall?

⊙  Did you give up?

⊙  How did you feel when you gave up?

⊙  Relieved, sad, angry, did you cry, happy, excited?

⊙  Did you push through?

⊙  How did you feel when you pushed through?

⊙  Were the emotions the same or did you feel as though you really accomplished something?

What have you discovered by doing this exercise? Are you more aware of how you operate when you have hit a barrier? I am asking you these questions because I want to create awareness for you. I want you to observe how you have handled obstacles previously.

If you have ever played golf you will know that there are so many obstacles. There are trees, branches from the trees (which are really annoying when you've clipped one after hitting the best shot of your life), posts, water, bunkers, lots of hazards, birds flying off with your ball: you name it, you can guarantee an obstacle. I have yet to mention actually learning how to play the game of golf itself, and what about the mind? You will encounter many mental hurdles because of what goes on in your head, whether you are learning or playing on the golf course.

When I was learning to play golf I would reduce my handicap quite significantly, and then I would hit a wall. That wall would be where my handicap would sit for a period of time. It was very frustrating, to say the least.

This is how it went. I dropped from 45 to 34 within a couple of months of learning to play. Then it just sat there for a few months. I then went from 34 to about 22 in one big bang in a couple of weeks, then it just plateaued for another few months. Then from 22 to 16 and my handicap stayed like that for about six months, dropped to 10 and hung around 8 for the next six months. Then, over that next year, dropped right down to 0.

The aim was to get down to scratch in two years. It took an extra year; I did it in three. Sure, it took an extra year. It took longer than I assumed it was going to take, but what I didn't realize was that it was tougher than I thought it was going to be. There were so many challenges: learning the skills, learning how to manage myself on the golf course whilst learning the skills, adjusting to playing with ladies in their sixties and seventies who were beating me (frustrating), overcoming my demons from my tennis career and learning a sport from knowing nothing and therefore having no experience.

It sounds great to be able to achieve a scratch handicap in three years but what most people didn't see was the hard work I put into it. I was one hundred per cent committed to achieving my goal. There were no excuses. I had my golf coach, who lived six hours' drive away. I was running a business plus I worked out a schedule for every hour of the day when I was able to practice, including what I was going to practice and how I was going to practice.

You see, when you are on a mission you get to work. You map out what you want to do and then take action. At times I had to adjust things along the way. I had to understand that the process was going to take longer than expected. I had to be patient and mentally handle less-athletic people than me scoring better than me. I was constantly analysing my game to make sure I was working on the right areas to achieve my goal.

In saying all of that the plateaus still occurred. Yes, I would hit the wall, I had obstacles. As you can see, I would sit on a certain handicap for a period of time.

Now I will say that I went from 45 to 18 purely from full-swing tuition. I did practise the other parts of my game as well, but my coach until that point only focused on the full swing. We didn't really pay much attention to the other areas of my game. I pretty much fumbled and figured out what to do.

But, going from 18 to 0 was due to the refinement of my short game. These are the finer parts of the game. Make a mental note of that for later.

Let's get back to the barriers.

The barriers occurred for four reasons:

1. My skills were not consistent.

2. My skills needed refinement.

3. My skills needed time to develop.

4. My mental skills were not up to par.

Now this was when it got really tough. To me, I wasn't seeing improvement and it was a hard slog. I felt like I wasn't getting anywhere even though I would show up every day and work on my skills and do what I needed to do to improve my game.

But after grinding it out day after day, and at times it would be months until I would have a breakthrough, I would finally break that handicap and drop to a new one.

But it wasn't just working on the physical skills that was creating the breakthroughs. Those mental demons from my tennis days were coming back to haunt me.

I had to get to work on my physical skills, refine them, work on them daily to make them consistent and allow time for them to develop, but I also had to get to work on my mental skills or lack thereof: I had to build that self-belief. I had to learn to trust my judgement and trust my swing. I had to develop structure and routines. I had to learn how to focus better and not allow distractions, other players' comments or opinions, or one bad shot or hole to hold me back from performing at my best. I had to learn how to manage my time and my mind better in training and in performance so that I would not tire out. I had to make sure I was mentally alert when I had to be in order to perform at my best.

When I had the idea to formulate the TM Sportykidz business I had no business experience. You can say that no business experience is a barrier but should you let that hold you back? No way!

There were three main skills I had at the time of piecing together this business. I had a university degree, which taught me how to teach sport, a tennis-teaching qualification and about four years of tennis-coaching experience. I didn't have skills in teaching every sport I was about to teach, but because I knew *how* to teach I knew I would be able to work it out.

What I designed was a formula for how to teach children sport so they would have lots of fun and learn at the same time. I would take the children through processes and progressions throughout each sport. It worked like a charm.

*But there were barriers in building the business.*

The first barrier was not knowing if anyone would attend the classes. I asked the question, 'Is there a need for this kind of program?' In the 1989 film *Field of Dreams* there was a scene where the character played by Kevin Costner was walking around in his cornfield and he kept hearing this whisper, 'If you build it, they will come.' My question about the business was, 'If I built it, would they come?' So rather than questioning whether they would come, I did market research. Rather than guess, I decided to find out if my idea was what the market wanted.

I approached five pre-schools to hand out questionnaires for the parents to fill out. Eureka. It was exactly what the parents were looking for. The very first barrier was overcome.

The second barrier was getting the business off the ground. I didn't have enough money to purchase equipment and I had no idea where I was going to run the program. I wrote out a business plan - again it wasn't perfect - made an appointment with the bank and applied for a business loan.

That was a lot of money for me at the time. I had just spent the previous two months in the United States of America exploring and having fun after I had finished my university degree. When I returned, I didn't have any work to come back to but I had some cash in the bank. To my surprise the bank approved my loan for $7000 and I was on my way.

The third barrier was that I had no clients to teach. No clients, no business. I visited every pre-school in the whole area where I live—the Northern Beaches in Sydney—to see what kind of response I would get so I could then determine the location. There were just under one hundred pre-schools. Perfect, I had a good response, but what was the location? I had enquiries coming in from the whole peninsula, so they couldn't all come to the same place as it would be too far to travel. Initially, I set up three specific locations the peninsula to make it convenient for the parents by giving them less travel time. Less travel time would ensure they would attend the classes (this is mentioned in the fourth barrier).

The fourth barrier I had was that I didn't know where I was going to run the program. I had the plan to teach certain sports on a tennis court and others on an oval. So I went and visited a few tennis centres and approached councils for teaching ovals and so on. Done. I secured three tennis centres and ovals to use for teaching, and the barrier was overcome.

The fifth barrier was deciding what I would teach in the actual program. I was excited because the clients were ready and I had secured locations, but how would I teach all the other sports that I hadn't taught before? As I mentioned earlier, I had a formula that worked. I had a few years of experience teaching tennis and had learned how to modify everything for little kids. That was the plan. I would follow that formula of how I taught little kids on the tennis court and apply the same knowledge to all the other sports.

Ka-pow! It worked!

It became a great business. It was really cool to start something from nothing and watch it grow into a successful enterprise.

Years later, starting an online business was another story. In the beginning there were barriers everywhere. I had absolutely no idea about websites, blog sites, social-media platforms, YouTube or internet marketing. Let alone how to shoot a video, how to edit videos, how to upload videos, what software was needed, how to market online, how to attract my target market and those are just a few to start with.

I didn't grow up with a computer. Back in the 'olden days', as my two nieces would say, computers were just starting to hit the market. They were very basic. When I was at university all I used a computer for was for writing assignments. There were no social-media sites around that time, there were some forums for communication but with my limited knowledge that's all I knew. Even leading up to me starting my business online, I tended to use the computer only to write my sports programs and send emails. That was it.

In the same way I approached golf and the sports-skills business, I knew that I had to learn what to do if I was going to make it all work in the online world. I bought courses on how to get a business up online. I discovered what I needed to put in place, for example, that I needed to create an online presence. I set up a few websites. I had the first one done professionally and I learned how to do the other two myself. I don't recommend you do it yourself though - it wastes too much time. That was me with my being 'Miss Independent I can do it all myself' type attitude.

Through research and getting assistance I identified the software and equipment needed, so then I was up and running.

Would you call them barriers?

For sure. I could have said, 'Well I don't know what to do here, I'm not techy, I am lost and overwhelmed, it's all too hard.' But I didn't let that stop me, I set out to learn and conquer.

You can say that was the first barrier—not knowing how to start online. I had no skills and no experience, but I had the thirst for knowledge to find out and make it work. I sought out help from experts. I always learn from those who have done it before. They understand what needs to be done and the challenges that will be faced. That's why it's important to get coaching from the beginning; to work with someone who has been there before makes a massive difference, so you know exactly what to do and you have someone who knows how to assist you in working you through the hurdles.

The second barrier I encountered was to find out, what were the most important elements to make an online business earn an income. I believe the most important reason for why you do something is because of your purpose and why you want to do it. The money will come if you get your foundations right.

Simon Sinek, who wrote *Start With Why* and *Leaders Eat Last,* talks about starting with 'your why', 'the purpose, cause, that inspires you to do what you do'. He believes you shouldn't make it about the money and I agree one hundred per cent. It's making the mind shift to believe in that. When you do that, money doesn't become the reason why you do something, but having money helps you to be able to do a lot more. Money is just a tool.

What I discovered was that in order to have a business online I needed to have a subscriber list. This list is the most important business asset that you will ever have online. This is Online Business 101, you must have a subscriber list.

I will give you a quick tip about your list and how you treat it. Your list is a group of people who follow you. I like to call them 'your tribe'. These people will follow you because they feel that you can show them the way. They look up to you. Treat them with respect, because they are not just a list of subscribers. They are real people, just like you and me. Remember that when you are sending your tribe an email—that email is landing in a very personal space, their inbox. Therefore, treat them with respect and they will do the same to you.

Work on creating a responsive list. It is better to have a small list that is highly responsive than a huge list that is unresponsive. I have had both. How to keep that list responsive is one simple word: 'relationship'. Work on building a relationship with your list. They will get to know you, like you and trust you. The KLT Factor: Know, Like and Trust. Always work on increasing the connection and relationship you have with your list.

The most challenging barrier online, I believe, especially when starting out, is knowing how to market to the tribe of people who follow you. When I started this online journey, I knew exactly what my market needed. However, what I didn't know was what they wanted.

*Big tip right there: I didn't know what they wanted!*

Yes I did research in the beginning when I was putting the business together, but I still thought I knew better. Again I will say it, *I knew what they needed, but not what they wanted.*

It took me about nine months of solid work to put my elaborate program for my new online business together. This program was to teach people how to play golf, and covered every single skill from a beginner level to get them up to a very proficient level at playing golf. I called it "Get Into The Swing". I was still working full time on my face-to-face golf-teaching business, so I would do this after work hours and on weekends. I will say it was an awesome program: I had step-by-step videos, step-by-step images, PDFs explaining all the steps, worksheets, practice sheets, I covered every single aspect so nothing was left behind.

Once the program was ready for launch, I was so excited. I thought, 'This is it, this is my breakthrough, I am going to reduce my actual golf-teaching hours, create more of the freedom I am looking for, create a huge income and get out of the sun.' When I launched the program I had six people participate. Four dropped out after a month and two stayed in it for about six months.

Two things ran through my mind at this point.

1. I was devastated because I thought I had failed and was a failure.

2. I was exhausted. I was so mentally exhausted because not only had the program taken nine months to bring together but I had actually been working on putting the online business together for fifteen months.

It was time to take some time out. I couldn't see straight nor think clearly so there was no point bashing my head against the wall.

After a number of months taking some time out (I took a year off from building the online golf business) the best decision I made was to survey my list. I asked my subscribers what they were looking for and what problems they had.

Ah, the light bulb appeared above my head. What I had discovered from this experience was a huge lesson in marketing.

I had been going about things in the wrong order. I needed to:

⊙ ask my tribe what they want,

⊙ cater to what they want, and

⊙ *then* show them what they need.

The message here, and I want you to get this very clear, is that you will always have barriers, but it is how you work through the barriers which is the key.

If you get anything out of this chapter make it this:

*You will always encounter obstacles!*

*It's how you work through the obstacles that is the key!*

## HOW ARE YOU GOING TO WORK THROUGH YOUR OBSTACLES?

Earlier in this chapter I asked you to write down the three biggest times you hit a wall.

I want you to now really work on the biggest obstacle that you are facing right now. It could be your sport, your business, your study, a relationship, anything that is having the biggest impact on your life right now.

Get out your journal and answer the questions below so that we can figure it out together, so you can take action rather than feeling like you are stuck.

Let's begin.

### STEP 1: WHAT IS YOUR BIGGEST OBSTACLE?

1. What is the biggest obstacle you are facing right now?

2. Why is it your biggest obstacle?

3. Why do you think it is stopping you from moving forward?

4. What are the emotions that are coming up for you about this obstacle? How do you feel?

5.   Are there any family or close relationships that are holding you back?

6.   If there are, why are they holding you back?

7.   Is there anything else that is holding you back? Give as much detail as you can here.

OK this is great. We are identifying what the obstacle is here.

## STEP 2: WHAT ARE THE CONSEQUENCES?

1.   What are the consequences of you hitting this obstacle? What do you think that you are missing out on because you have hit this obstacle?

2.   How does it make you feel because you are missing out?

3.   Is missing out because you have hit this obstacle affecting anyone else around you?

4.   How does it make them feel?

This is great because we are identifying that you are feeling like you are missing out, which is causing you to feel some pain and discomfort. We need to feel this because this will be what we use to push us forward.

## STEP 3: IF YOU CONTINUE DOWN THIS PATH THEN WHAT?

1.   If you continue down this path of feeling like you are missing out, what will happen to you?

2.   Will you have any regrets?

3.   Will you let yourself down?

4. Will you let your family and loved ones down?

5. What else will happen?

## STEP 4: USE THIS TO FUEL YOU

Use this step as fuel to help you to move forward and work through your obstacles. Use the discomfort or pain that you are feeling to figure out what you now need to do. What are the questions you need to ask yourself? The questions following are to prompt you. Use these or ask your own.

1. What do I need to do to work through this obstacle?

2. What are the skills I need to learn?

3. What courses do I need to do?

4. Who do I need to speak to who will help me?

5. Who can I role model? Who has been through what I am going through?

6. How much do I want to work through this obstacle?

7. Who is relying on me to work through this obstacle?

8. Why do I want to work through this obstacle, what will it do for me, what will it do for others?

9. When am I going to get started and work through this obstacle?

Awesome, this is fantastic. You are now starting to think for yourself. You are becoming resourceful and working through your biggest obstacle right now. Congratulate and be proud of yourself because you have it all there deep inside of you. You just have to dig in and find it.

# CHAPTER 7

# KEEPiNG YOUR EYE ON THE BALL
# THE ESSENTiAL HABiTS

*'I've learned that it's not a straight road to the top, and there are going to be setbacks along the way. You have to be patient, and you have to keep believing in what you're doing. And keep believing in yourself, no matter what is happening. And then eventually you'll get there. – Eugenie Bouchard*

## KEEPiNG YOUR EYE ON THE BALL

'Keeping your eye on the ball' refers to you staying focused, being patient, having discipline, being dedicated, having determination, to persisting and to never giving up no matter what.

Of course it is easy to get distracted and become disillusioned. Especially when you discover that pursuing your ultimate dream isn't as easy as you thought it was going to be. It is tough, there is so much work involved. Some days are fantastic and you are up in the clouds, everything is flowing, you are seeing that the effort you are putting into your dream is showing results. Other days are so hard that you question whether this is the right thing for you, as you can't see a way out. You are slogging it away, grinding it out, there are no rewards, you question whether you are making any progress at all, there is no light at the end of the tunnel—that tunnel is pitch black and you can't see a thing. Then you have the days in between where there is some progress. It is slow progress but at least you feel as though you are moving forward even if it is slow; at least you feel that you are doing something, going somewhere, not standing still or feeling as though you are going backwards.

In anything that you do, whether you play sport, study, have your own business or work on a career in a company, the most important thing you MUST KNOW, is that you DON'T STOP and NEVER TAKE YOUR EYE OFF THE BALL!

It's like when you are out on the tennis court. What happens if you take your eye off the ball? You miss the ball completely. You lose the point, you lose the set and lose the match. You must keep your focus and keep working. It's one shot at a time.

I love it when the top tennis players, such as Roger Federer, are interviewed. Federer is usually asked by a journalist in a pre tournament interview something along the lines of, 'how do you think you will go playing against Nadal in the final?' Roger replies something along the line of, 'we are only in the first round, we have more matches to go, I am only focusing on my next match, I need to get through that one first.'

What is Roger saying? He is informing the reporters that he is focused on his next match, his next job. He is aware that he could come up against Nadal in the final, but he knows he has to do the work to get there first. Therefore, his focus is on playing his next match, playing his best to win and to continuing the process until he reaches the final. He is not looking ahead because he understands that he has to focus on what he needs to do first. Not what he will do a week later.

Roger understands that if he focuses and gives one hundred per cent of himself in his next match and subsequent, matches he will get to the final. But he needs to stay focused, be committed, patient, persistent and not give up, just keep going.

It is the same in golf. You also have to keep your eye on the ball, keep focused. Actually, you can hit a golf ball with your eyes closed. When I teach golf, I have my clients close their eyes and swing. They are surprised at how they can actually hit a ball without looking at it.

The power in that is staying in the moment and trusting your swing. Which is really trusting yourself. You can keep your focus without watching what you have to do; it is a matter of trust. It is trusting that all the work you have done will give you the result. As long as you trust the process and do the work you can create it. Yes, even a golf swing with your eyes closed!

## WHEN IT GETS TOUGH!

When it gets tough, and it will, you will need to dig deep within and work through all the obstacles thrown at you. You now understand that there are obstacles because we discussed it in the last chapter and you have identified your biggest obstacle. But you will need habits in place to get through your obstacles.

## BEING PATIENT – DO I HAVE TO?

You bet you do. You are going to have to have patience if you want to achieve your ultimate dream. I encounter so many people who constantly tell me how impatient they are, how they have to have it happen now, how will if it doesn't happen straight away they become bored, and how they can't sit still for more than thirty seconds.

What?

Obviously these people haven't played much sport. There is so much that sport teaches you, there are so many valuable lessons you can learn from it, but one of the big ones is definitely patience.

Golf, whether you like it or not, teaches you patience. I always invite people to learn or play golf because it is one of those sports that really brings up your vulnerabilities. It is a really powerful way for you to learn so much about yourself and how you handle everything that is thrown at you.

When I took up golf I thought I could get to scratch in two years, you have heard the story. I thought golf would be a cinch because I was a highly skilled sportsperson, who had competed overseas in tennis and was always in the top teams for all the other sports at school.

You don't have to move to hit a golf ball, so it would definitely be easier than playing tennis. In tennis you are dictated to by your opponent whereas in golf you are the one in total control.

I thought it was a no-brainer.

I thought I could stand on the practice range and hit the balls off the ground and they would soar through the air, just like Tiger Woods. Tiger makes it look so easy!

That was an education in itself.

What I realized was that I was starting a new sport from the beginning. I didn't know a thing about golf. Absolutely nothing. This was when the learning curve arrived. It was a very steep learning curve too, I might add.

When I teach people golf I always say to them, 'golf is a game of feeling awkward until you feel comfortable with feeling awkward.' Then I say, 'welcome to golf.' I know what they are going to go through but they are not yet aware of it. Fortunately for them, I have been down the path they are about to embark on. If they decide to stick it out, they won't be alone, they will get an expert to guide them through the journey much more effectively and efficiently. If they do choose to go it alone, it's a much more challenging path, and my advice is to choose the other option.

Golf is so unnatural. It is not as easy as it looks. It has many challenges, both physically with positioning, and mentally—if you have played golf you will understand. If you haven't yet, then perhaps you could even go to a driving range and hit a bucket of balls—it will be an eye-opener and you will comprehend what I am talking about.

What I discovered about golf was that I had to pay my dues and be incredibly patient. My golf game wasn't going to appear overnight or straight after picking up the golf club.

I understood I had to practise and work on all of the skills. I felt that I had a slight advantage over other new golfers because I had taught other sports. I identified that learning how to play golf was essential to me, therefore it was important to take golf lessons from a coach, plus I knew that applying myself to do the work was imperative (because I had been down that road before with tennis). That I understood. But what I soon realized was that it wasn't as easy as it looked: this expectation of it all just happening quickly and falling into place because I showed up for lessons and practice was completely unrealistic.

That was the discovery. This game of golf was not so easy and it was going to require a lot of dedication and hard work. What I also identified was that at times, even if I practised for twelve hours in a day, I wouldn't see the result of all my hard work the next day. Even when I attended a practice session the next day, I couldn't remember how I did it the day before and felt as if I had to start all over again. It took weeks of practising and refining, sometimes months, to see an improvement.

This is exactly the same in life and in everything else you will tackle in your career.

What about weight loss? Many people in the world, as you are aware, go down the path of 'it's time to lose weight'. They then start doing some exercise and changing their eating habits. All positive. However, the problem is that they expect a change in their weight on the scales overnight and if nothing has changed at all within seven days, then 'this weight-loss thing' doesn't work. They give up. Weight loss is the same as learning to play golf, it sometimes takes weeks and even months to see significant results.

I always hear people talk about their weight when I am out for a coffee or dinner with friends. It comes up everywhere. Yet people will talk and talk about it but do nothing about it. Why?

Because it's challenging. They have to change their eating habits, the body fat doesn't just melt off the bone and the reality is, they are simply not dedicated enough to make the change, because it will require dedication, patience, focus, attention to detail, persistence and a never-give-up attitude. They want it, but not bad enough. I don't want to sound rude but it is the truth.

People will only work on losing weight if they have a life-threatening illness, they are going to get married, to impress a partner, to get a date or for something other than for themselves. Actually, most of the time, we won't do something that feels as though it is painful and hard because it's too difficult, we really don't want it bad enough.

Often I hear the weight conversation, 'Oh, I should lose weight, blah, blah, blah' but twelve months down the track I hear the same conversation again.

I never had a weight problem being a sportsperson until I became less active. When I started teaching golf I didn't have to be as active, because I walk around and check players' techniques and work on refining them etc. but I am not physically 'doing' like I did in tennis coaching, they are doing the work, I am just guiding them.

When I started teaching I noticed I started to put on some weight. Mmmm, what's going on and how did that happen? I had developed some not-so-good habits around food that I could get away with it before, but no longer. I also thought because I was getting older it was getting harder. You hear this said all the time, 'the older you get the harder it is to lose weight', and the body just keeps adding weight on.

I will disagree. I have always disagreed with that one. It doesn't matter how old you are, you can lose weight, you can play sport, train at the gym and achieve any dream that you want to pursue.

*Never be limited by someone else's opinion!*

You know it is not that hard to lose weight and to keep the weight off if you really want to do that, the choice is yours. You just need to have habits in place such as patience, dedication, persistence, a never-give-up attitude, discipline and focus. It is all up to you.

Yes, I had added a few extra kilograms to my body: I was ten kilos heavier than when I got married to my lovely hubby. How did that happen?

I wasn't really paying much attention, to be honest. I was just doing my thing, teaching golf, training at the gym and eating like I was still playing professional sport, yet I wasn't training like a professional sportsperson. I have to give credit here to my chiropractor. We had a long discussion about my weight frustration, and with just a few simple tweaks to what I was doing, ten kilos came off.

It wasn't a quick-fix process. It required dedication, patience, attention to detail and focus. It took about three months to take off about five kilos and then it took another six months or so to knock off the rest, but I did it still eating some of the yummy foods like chocolate, lollies and desserts.

I will never let the kilos come back on again, simply because I know and understand how to manage myself and my habits. I have the dedication and the focus to ensure I don't have to go through that again. Yet, people around me who watched it happen, still talk about how they should lose weight blah, blah, blah!

They will never lose the weight unless they have a reason to. It will remain all talk.

The point of this story is not about losing weight. It is the fact that you can do anything as long as you have patience, you are dedicated, you are focused, you are determined, you are driven, you are persistent and you don't give up on you.

You see, it is not just about having the patience. It is a whole combination of habits and behaviours that will help you achieve your big-ass dream.

◎

In your journal, write down these questions and answer them.

1. Am I a patient person?

2. If yes, why am I patient, if no why am I not patient?

3. What do I need to do to ensure I am patient and focused on achieving my dream?

## DO I NEED TO HAVE DiSCiPLiNE?

What does having discipline mean to you?

To me it means having a plan in place, having a daily structure, focusing on what needs to be done during that day that will get me to my goals and dreams. Of course there is persistence and that never-give-up attitude, as there will be obstacles that come up, but, it's having the discipline to work on that dream every day that will lead you to success.

It is so easy to be distracted, life can get in the way, but it doesn't have to if you don't let it.

Look at the distractions around you today. The biggest one is the mobile phone. It is a mini computer and we can do just about anything we want on it at any given moment of the day. Powerful tool, right? It is amazing the technology that we have today.

However, it can also be what holds us back from moving forward because sometimes we seem to be controlled by it rather than us controlling it.

I found the following experience very interesting. I caught the bus home after attending a course in the CBD of Sydney. I was travelling backwards, facing most of the other passengers, and I was looking at these eight people who were sitting in front of me. Each one of them was on their phone. Yes, I was too. I was listening to a podcast about motivation. I'm not sure what the man opposite me was listening to, but the others were playing games or on social media. Easy distraction, right? It's right there at our fingertips.

When you are disciplined you are not distracted. When you have a plan and a structure to your day you are not distracted. *But how can you be disciplined and not be distracted?*

Easy! Don't put yourself in a place where you can be distracted. Set yourself up for success, don't set yourself up for distraction.

There are simple things you can do that will make all the difference.

Here are some examples to minimize the distractions:

⊙ Set your phone to aeroplane mode to avoid distracting notifications.

⊙ Set a timer on your phone so that you can focus on a specific task, training session or study session and only that task, training session or study session.

⊙ Only check your phone for messages and phone calls in between or after your set specific task, training session or study session and not during the specific task, training session or study session.

That's pretty simple, isn't it? If you were just to do some things as simple as those above, it would make all the difference in your focus.

Did you know that if you get distracted when you are working on a specific task, training session or study session, that it could take you up to twenty minutes to get re-focused again?

Now if you are constantly being distracted then you can't focus on what needs to be done, and when you can't focus, you don't get the ideal results you are after. You become frustrated, disillusioned and can even get to the point of giving up, because it all gets too hard. The simple thing you need to do is to minimize the distractions.

I showed you above some simple strategies to lessen the distractions, but this is where the discipline kicks in. You have to have the discipline to put it in place and follow that structure because if you don't you will again be back into distraction mode.

*Do you have the discipline to be able to do something as easy as that?*

In sport you have to be disciplined because if you don't you will be beaten. It won't matter if you are in a team sport or competing individually, you will require discipline. You will need to have the patience to learn the skills of that sport and you will have to make the time to practise and refine those skills so that you can make them work under pressure when you are competing in a tournament. But it will be up to you to make that happen.

To even give myself a chance to travel overseas to play tennis professionally or play to a golf handicap of scratch required me to be disciplined. I had to show up each day even when I didn't feel like it. I had to grind it out when it was really tough and I couldn't see any improvements—that's discipline. It's not about showing up and hoping that you will have wonderful moments all the time—it is not possible. It's all the work that you do that will lead you to having those wonderful moments. It's about having the courage and the discipline to show up when it's tough, when it's hard, when you don't want to do it and when you don't feel like it. All this work you are doing will make you stronger, will build your character into the person that you want to become.

Think of it this way. It's like you have a bank account, but instead of money being in there, it's the daily discipline of you showing up every day to do the work on your dream. Every time you show up and do the work, you make a deposit into your bank. If you do it regularly those deposits grow, just like money in an account. Every time you deposit money into the bank, you can see your money grow.

When it comes time to compete in a tournament, because of those regular deposits you have made, you can withdraw them from your bank and perform the way you want to. Why? Because you have had the discipline to show up and train, you have had the discipline to do the work. You can draw on it because you have the skills in place, again because you have disciplined yourself to work on achieving your dream.

When people have had golf lessons with me, they want results but they don't have the discipline to practise. They don't make the time to practise. They want the results but are not willing to do the work, because they simply will not structure themselves. Sounds simple, doesn't it? Practise what you learn, and keep practising, so that when you have your next lesson you can tweak what needs to be tweaked and you can work on the next phase. The typical answer is, 'I haven't had time to practise!' It's not that you haven't had time to practise, it is the fact that you haven't disciplined yourself to schedule a time to practise.

I am the same with practising the guitar. I want to practise but I am not spending the time practising, because I am not scheduling the time in to do it. Therefore, I am not disciplined enough to make the effort.

*Discipline Requires Effort!*

*If you don't make the effort you won't have the discipline!*

In your journal, write down these questions and answer them.

1.  Am I a disciplined person?

2.  If yes, why am I disciplined, if no why am I not disciplined?

3.  What do I need to do to ensure I am disciplined and focused on achieving my dream?

## HOW DEDICATED OR COMMITTED ARE YOU REALLY?

We have talked about being patient and disciplined, but how dedicated or how committed are you?

When you are pursuing a dream, you can't just think that one day this is what I want and hope the next day it lands in your lap. Nothing works like that. Not goals or dreams. Perhaps if you order takeaway you can do that, but not when it comes to creating your destiny.

We talked in our very first chapter about having one-hundred-per-cent belief in you to make your dream happen. No belief in you, and you won't achieve your dream. And as well as belief, you will need to apply yourself to your dream. You will need to be committed to your dream.

I won't sugar-coat this for you, but I am not trying to put you off pursuing your dream either. I want you to go after your dream and go get it. I just want to make you aware that you will need to have habits and systems in place that will get you to where you want to go.

I want you to take a few moments to think about what commitment means to you.

Commitment is a very serious word because this word alone will ensure whether you are successful in your sport, in your career, in your business and in life. You can't go into business and say I will 'give it a go' or 'give it a try', it's just like saying this about life: 'Oh I will give it a go.'

Get out your journal and before you continue reading on about commitment, I want you to write down what commitment means to you.

Write down the heading, 'What commitment means to me' and the answer below. Once you have written out what commitment means to you, then we will continue.

If you only get one thing out of this book today, then I want it to be sticking this word *commitment* deep into your subconscious.

When you take up golf, you are either in or you are out. Golf is one of those sports that you have to commit to learning if you want to do it well. If you want to hack yourself around the golf course, swiping at the ball and just hoping it will all come together with a lack of real commitment to learning it, then you will most likely not continue. You will say it is too hard and that you can't play it. If you haven't committed to learning the game, you won't know how to play or how to produce a good consistent swing, and it will be no wonder that you carve up the fairways with so many divots!

When I took up golf at the age of thirty-four, there was no way that I was going to get into this sport by just showing up to play on the day. I knew if I wanted to play at a high level, I was going to have to commit to lessons, commit to practising, commit to mental training, commit to gym training, commit to eating the right food and commit to learning how to play on the golf course.

So that's what I did. On my days off I would practise twelve hours a day. The days I worked I would usually do two hours before work, sneak in half an hour at lunch time when possible, and then finish with two hours of training at the end of the day.

I don't tell you this to impress you. I want to impress *upon* you that I was committed to learning golf and I am sharing my level of commitment. I was all in.

When I started all of my businesses, my sports-skills business, tennis- and golf-coaching businesses, and my online business I was all in, one hundred per cent. As I mentioned earlier, I am not here to give it a go and see if it works out, I commit one hundred per cent and give all I have to everything I do.

## WHAT IS COMMiTMENT?

The word commitment is defined as the state or quality of being dedicated to a cause, activity, etc. Commitment is about giving your word or your promise to be consistent with your actions. It is the discipline that carries you across the bridge when at times you don't feel like doing it.

Warren Buffet, an American business magnate, investor and philanthropist says to, 'Invest in as much of yourself as you can, you are your one biggest asset by far.'

When you read that quote what comes to mind?

For me it is about devoting time and learning into you and discovering who you really are. Once you are clear on who you are and what you stand for, you can commit to whatever you set your mind to pursuing in life. You are the most important human being here on this planet. If you can look after you and work on being the best you can be, then you can do more and help more people around you. Those are powerful words.

Tony Robbins, a life strategist, personal-finance instructor and self-help author says:

> 'I believe life is constantly testing us for our level of commitment, and life's greatest rewards are reserved for those who demonstrate a never-ending commitment to act until they achieve. This level of resolve can move mountains, but it must be constant and consistent. As simplistic as this may sound, it is still the common denominator separating those who live their dreams from those who live in regret.'

The truth about commitment is that we either commit to something that we are passionate about or we just go through the motions. If we are passionate, we can't wait to wake up in the morning, dive out of bed and tackle the day with eagerness.

If we are just going through the motions it can be incredibly dissatisfying and can leave you exhausted and stressed out.

Do you remember how you felt about going to school? I still do! If you don't enjoy school or work, in the mornings when you have to show up at work or school, you struggle to get out of bed—actually the stress and dread is there from the night before. You dread tomorrow arriving. You can't sleep, you feel restless, you toss and turn in bed then when the alarm goes off, you are so tired that you keep hitting the snooze button on your alarm. You leave it until the last possible moment to get out of bed, you see the time on the clock and then you are left with no choice, you have to get up because otherwise you will be late. Your only motivation to get out of bed is so you don't get in trouble at school for lateness, or so you can get paid to pay the bills and support your family or yourself. You are not overly fussed about being at school or work but you do it because you have no other choice.

My niece, Evelyn, had been going through that too. At ten years of age. On Sunday mornings when she woke up, she would say, 'Oh, my weekend is over, I have to go to school tomorrow.' I remember that too well myself.

She doesn't feel that way now, she is excited about school because she is playing soccer for the school team and on the weekends. It is all she talks about. She is committed to being a better soccer player and learning the skills. School just happens to be part of the process because if she goes to school she gets to play soccer.

The first step to commitment is to make a promise that you can keep. It's simple, isn't it? I will say it again: Make a promise you can keep.

Sir Richard Branson, a businessman and investor, is best known as the founder of the Virgin Group, which comprises more than 400 companies. He says in his book *Let's Not Screw It, Let's Just Do It*, that from childhood he had been taught by his parents that promises were important and should be kept. His parents said that if you couldn't keep a promise then y make one. Sir Richard is grateful for that grounding and that is why he sticks to is his word.

Sir Richard sets his goals and sticks to them and firmly believes that success is more than luck, just as I am sharing with you in this chapter and this book. Success is not about just waking up one day and hoping that you can achieve your dream.

There is much more required than simply having a dream or an idea. You have to have the ability to commit and pursue your dream. As you can see, in order for you to accomplish what you want in your life, you will have to make a commitment.

*What kind of commitment are you ready to make?*

*Are you ready to make a one-hundred-per-cent commitment?*

It's important that you understand how you operate. What do I mean by this?

We are creatures of habits and patterns. So when it comes to commitment you will have patterns that you will be able to backtrack throughout your life, usually stemming from your childhood. That's where we get the grounding for how to function in life.

Here are some examples of various commitment levels:

- ⊙ You may be someone who gives everything, gives it all, but at the first sign of failure or disappointment you quit.

- ⊙ You may be someone who doesn't commit to anything, therefore you avoid the C word, Commitment.

- ⊙ You may be someone who commits to a new project every week.

- ⊙ You maybe someone who commits to something wholeheartedly but you may leave the back door open so if something better comes along, you will move on.

- ⊙ You may be someone who commits one hundred per cent and you keep going until you get what you want.

In your journal write out these questions and answer them.

1. How committed am I to pursuing my dream?

2. How much do I want this dream?

3. Am I committed to doing the work?

4. Am I committed to making a plan?

5. Am I committed to believing in me one hundred per cent?

6. Am I committed to learning the skills required?

7. Am I committed to practising the skills?

8. Am I committed to working through the obstacles?

9. Am I committed to being patient?

10. Am I committed to being structured?

11. Am I committed to being disciplined?

12. Am I committed to being focused?

13. Am I committed to being persistent?

14. Am I committed to never giving up?

Questions 3 to 14 must have a YES! This is what it is going to take. You will need everything you can give to achieve your dream, because it will require all that you can give.

If you can't, then I suggest you look for something else that you can call your everything!

## HOW PERSiSTENT WiLL YOU NEED TO BE?

Being persistent is about not giving up when it gets tough. We have spoken about obstacles that will come up. You have identified what your biggest obstacle is whilst you have been working through this book.

How persistent will you need to be to work on your dream when a challenge comes up or you hit a brick wall?

Some will say this is all too hard, I just can't get through this, but what will you say?

When I had been playing golf for three years it was decided that I should do a golf traineeship. A golf traineeship is a training program to prepare you to run a pro shop and teach golf at a golf club. I agreed to go through the process. It wasn't ideally what I was working towards but it was suggested to me by a golf professional who I was working with at the time and I took his professional advice.

So here I am, thirty-seven years of age, fronting up to a playing test with eighteen-year-old men. We had to play fifty-four holes for the playing test. The first day we played eighteen holes and the second day we played thirty-six holes. I was so nervous I couldn't think straight. I kept heading off to the bathroom before we teed off as I was hyperventilating and I didn't want anyone to see what I was going through. I had never experienced that before any tournament I had ever played in either tennis or golf.

All I could do was focus on my breathing, work on keeping myself calm in between shots and talk to myself about staying focused in the moment when I played each shot throughout the round. It was mentally gruelling. But I kept hanging in there. I had a relatively good score, and I qualified for the traineeship.

Great. I was persistent and kept working at it throughout that playing test.

However, throughout the year it was getting really tough. I was working full-time in the pro shop, I had my sports-skills business where I had some staff working for me, I was doing some tennis coaching on the side, plus I had weekly assignments due for the traineeship and was in a terrible personal relationship. Somewhere along the line I also had to fit in practice so I could perform at the level required to stay in the traineeship.

Well something had to give and give it did. I failed the playing side of the traineeship in that first year. My average was a bit higher than what was required, but in saying that, I was playing my best golf in the last six months of that first year, whereas in the first six months I was a disaster. I felt out of my depth. I felt like I was a tennis player trying to be a golfer. I had a lot going through my mind at the time but I was still persistent and hanging in there.

So yes, I failed! But you know what? I didn't give up. I found another way to become a golf coach. I didn't let this one organisation or this one major event in my life hold me back from pursuing what I wanted at the time.

I share this story with you because I want you to know that just because you have an event or an obstacle that crops up in front of you and stops you from achieving, you don't let that stop you. You keep persisting and you keep working through it and look for another way to achieve your goals.

There is not just one way to achieve your dream. You just have to work and figure out the way in which *you* can get there.

In your journal, write out these questions and answer them.

1.  What does being persistent mean to me?

2.  Can I hang in there and keep going no matter what type of obstacles I face?

3.  Will I seek out guidance when I get stuck and don't know what to do?

4.  Whose guidance will I seek out?

5.  Are there particular habits I must have in place to keep me persistent?

6.  What are these habits I must have or introduce to keep me working towards my dream?

7.  Are there particular systems I must have in place to keep me persistent?

8.  What are these systems I must have or introduce to keep me working towards my dreams?

9.  Who is my role model or who are my role models that I can use to keep me focused and persistent in pursuing my dream?

Not sure how to answer these questions around the habits and systems you need in place? Don't fear, you don't need to know all the answers. It's all about figuring out who you are, what you are capable of and when you can get coaching, mentorship and guidance.

It's all about becoming more aware of what you want, how you operate and how you can achieve your dreams in your life.

# DON'T LET PERFECTiON HOLD YOU BACK

There is a great book written by Dr Bob Rotella, *Golf Is A Game Of Not Perfect*.

I have to admit I am a perfectionist when it comes to sport. My attitude is that if you are mechanically efficient in a skill then you have the potential to perform at your maximum level.

But being a perfectionist can really hold you back.

When I was learning to play golf, I was working on the perfect swing. My coach used to get quite frustrated with me, as I was wanting it to be perfect. I would diligently practise all the drills, day in and day out. He would constantly be saying, 'Stop trying to get it so perfect.' I was a sportsperson, that's all I knew. If I could make skills as perfect as I could, they wouldn't break down in tournaments. Nothing wrong with that.

What did make me different though, to other perfectionists in the world, was the fact that I would still put myself out there in the game and continue to work on improving in a tournament, even if my swing really wasn't right.

I remember getting ready to play a particular tournament. I had changed coaches only a week before and my new coach had started to change my swing only a few days earlier. When was the perfect day to change the swing? Well, with many tournaments coming up over the year, the time was never going to be perfect. Therefore we began the changes.

Well, come the first tournament day it was not pretty. I sliced every single tee shot into the next fairway, which meant I would have to fight my way back onto my own fairway and find a way to get the ball down onto the green. This was character building. I couldn't wait to get down to the green where at least I could chip and putt; it was a relief to get there. That was the story for the rest of that week.

The following week it was the opposite. Every tee shot would now hook into the trees. Again I just couldn't wait to get to the green, relieved that all I had to do was sink a putt. Another character building week.

The point here from both of those tournaments is that I didn't wait until my swing was perfect before I entered the tournament. I did it all right in the middle of swing changes. When you go through a swing change you get caught between the old and the new swing movements. Not a great place to be, but you have no choice but to work through it and develop it along the way.

There was a lady, Mary, who I used to teach golf to a few years ago and she wanted to be a really good golfer. She too was a perfectionist.

Now Mary would have private lessons, attend clinics and show up to play on the course but would never compete in a competition. Her attitude was that if she could consistently shoot 36 stableford points—playing to her handicap—or better every time she played golf in practice, then she would start to compete in competitions.

Now if you look at the professional golfers in a four-day tournament, they may shoot 62 one day, 75 the next, 65 on the third day and 70 strokes on the last day. If you look at the scores they are not the same. And the professional golfers practise eight to twelve hours per day.

So this client of mine, Mary, was waiting for perfection before she would compete in a competition.

What do you think happened to Mary?

That's right, Mary never competed in a competition. She even left the golf club and hardly ever plays golf. Do you think Mary's expectations were too high?

If you are waiting for everything to be perfect, then you will never really begin. How long does it take for everything to be perfect?

I believe it is forever, because you will never feel that everything is right.

When starting my sports-skills business I had a plan, but the plan wasn't perfect. I didn't know where I was going to teach nor how I was going to teach the other sports. But I sought out locations.

I tested out the format of the program I was writing for the business and refined the teaching plan as I went. I identified what worked in the program and what didn't work. But because there was action being taken I could refine and develop the program as I went along. If I had waited until it was perfect then I could still be working on it to this very day and may never have started.

When I launched my business online, as I have mentioned before, I didn't know how to start or where to start. So many things to do and so many skills to learn. It can be incredibly overwhelming. I had launched a few websites and they were not great 'well the ones I had set up myself.' The site I had professionally done was really well done. Even though the sites I set up were not great to look at, it was a start and I knew over time I could change them and make them look more professional. It was important to get them up online so I could start writing blog posts and producing videos.

Videos can be daunting. When I shot my first video, it was so weird. I was looking into this camera with no one around (I didn't want anyone to hear what I was talking about), just in case they laughed at me. It was because I felt so uncomfortable with it. I reviewed the first video  and then shot it again. I must have done that about five times. I was highly critical of how I looked and how I pronounced words and whether I made sense and got my point across.

After about five videos I decided that it was time to make a decision. I had to stop being so critical because I realized that none of my videos would ever be perfect, I wasn't going to be polished when I spoke and I wanted people who watched my videos to see that this is the real me. I wanted people to connect with me for me, not for trying to be someone I was not. Therefore the decision was made to not be concerned about being perfect, to learn from making mistakes and let people accept me for who I am. If they didn't, then they were not the type of people I wanted to attract into my life.

The other point here was that I was taking action. My mission was to learn how I could inspire and have an impact on people.  I could continue to refine my videos and the way I conducted myself in front of the camera. I became less nervous and I got my points across in the videos better and more effectively. Instead of being critical about what I was producing I was better off getting feedback by analysing them.

You have to accept that you are not perfect at everything that you do, especially when you first start, but you have to get started and then you can fix it along the way. I had a client who wouldn't do a video until she was perfect at doing it. Sarah would write out her notes and would have to read out her notes to the video. If it wasn't right she would delete and start again. Sarah too admitted that she was a perfectionist. She compared herself with me, as she said I looked natural and gave clear and concise points in my videos. I reminded Sarah that I had done hundreds of videos and when I first started I too felt the same as her.

Sarah then agreed that if she just started doing them, she would get better. She acknowledged that in order for her to get better, she had to begin and then she could grow and develop from her first video. Sarah also decided not to be so critical of herself and built up her confidence with her videos, because she had been taking action, letting go of the perfectionism.

You won't know when the right moment will be because you are not prepared to put yourself out there. You can't create opportunities if everything has to be perfect.

Stop questioning whether your actions are perfect, get it out there and refine it along the way.

Jack Canfield, in his book *The Success Principles*, discusses using feedback to benefit your action taking. It's not about waiting for everything to be lined up in a row and only moving forward when everything is in place. When you start to take action you will get feedback along the way. The feedback you receive will give you data, advice, help, suggestions, direction, even criticisms, that will continually help you adjust and progress forward. The most important point from this is that once you get feedback you need to respond to it, not react to it.

You have to look at feedback to see whether you are taking the right actions and making the right decisions to give you the results you desire. Feedback is a mechanism that will help you make decisions in what your next steps will be. We discussed this in a previous chapter, about learning from mistakes and getting feedback.

It's not about how perfect you are, it is the fact that you are taking action.

In your journal, write these questions out and answer them.

1. Am I waiting for everything to be perfect before I am take action?

2. Why am I waiting for everything to be perfect?

3. Am I worried that I will be judged and criticized if what I am doing is not perfect?

4. Do I really care what others think of me?

5. Is there anything else that is holding me back?

6. What must I do today that is not so perfect but that I can just get on with?

## NEVER EVER GiViNG UP

Never give up on you and never give up on your dream. Give it your all, give everything you have got, exhaust all the avenues you can, because you don't want to live your life with regret.

I say this to you from my own personal experience with my tennis. I have come to terms with never having achieved the great heights I deeply wanted to achieve, but the regret I have is that I gave up too early on my dream. I was only twenty years old when I gave up on my dream. It took me from the age of twenty to forty-five to come to terms with never achieving what I wanted.

That's twenty-five years!

That's twenty-five years of holding onto what I didn't accomplish. That's twenty-five years of living with regret. You can't imagine the disrespect I had for myself over that time, simply because I gave up on me so early in my career and my life. At twenty years of age you are still a baby. At the time you think you are much older and mature but when you get to being forty-seven years old as I am now, you realize how much you didn't know and how young and raw you were in the world.

If you are twenty now and reading this, do not be offended as you will discover as you get older how young twenty really is. But, use it to your advantage. Take that youth you have and go for it, never give up on your dream. Keep pushing through and keep figuring out the way to make it happen no matter what is being thrown at you.

If you are older like me, I know you get it. You may have regrets like I did. You may have had a dream that you gave up on like I did. But that doesn't mean you can't go after what you want now. Don't let anything hold you back. Sure, you may have more responsibilities now, a family, a mortgage, a pressured job, but if you really want to make the changes in your life and go after what you really want, you can!

It will take a lot of effort and work. Any changes you make require effort, time, persistence, dedication, commitment and patience, but, if you really want it, like really want it, you can make it happen.

I have new dreams I want and a new drive to achieve. I now feel as though I have just turned twenty years old, but my advantage is that I have so much more experience. I can figure things out and if I don't know the answers I go and find out the answers. I go exploring, I ask questions, I do courses, I have a mentor. Nothing will hold me back and I will never give up.

This is why I say this to you:

*DON'T EVER GIVE UP ON YOU!*
*DON'T EVER GIVE UP ON YOUR DREAM!*
*KEEP PUSHING – KEEP STRIVING!*

I could share many stories with you about not giving up on other things I have done or what other athletes and entrepreneurs have done. However, I get the feeling now you get it! You get not to give up. You get that you have to keep pushing. You get that you have to keep striving. I know you get it!

In your journal, write these questions out and answer them.

1. What does never giving up mean to me?

2. What do I need to have in place so that I never give up on me?

3. Do I need to get mentorship or coaching so I never give up on me?

4. Who is my inspiration so that I never give up on me?

5. When it gets all too hard and I feel like I am going to just give it all up, who am I going to speak with to talk through all my worries and concerns?

6. What are the consequences I will face if I give up on my dream?

Never feel alone or that you are alone. There are people out there in the world who are there for you. Don't keep it all inside. Talk to people you trust and that you know are on your side. They will understand and be there for you.

*Give all you have and never give up on you!*

## CHAPTER 8

# CONSISTENCY – BEING CONSISTENT

*'In baseball, my theory is to strive for consistency, not to worry about the numbers. If you dwell on statistics you get shortsighted, if you aim for consistency, the numbers will be there at the end.'* – Tom Seaver

## THE EFFECT CALLED 'THE COMPOUND EFFECT'

If you want that ultimate dream you will need to be consistent. For example, if you look at a top professional golfer's swing, let's say Adam Scott's, what do you notice about his it? It is always the same. The setup, the positioning, the motion of the swing, it is always the same. That is consistency.

This is my absolute favourite talking about—consistency—as I am an expert at this. In simple terms, being consistent is how you make a habit of success.

A habit can be defined as a routine of behaviour that is repeated regularly and tends to occur unconsciously. It's a behaviour that is formed.

Think about Adam Scott's golf swing again. Adam's golf swing is on plane and would be regarded as one of the most technically correct golf swings in the world.

How did Adam get a swing like that?

People say it was because his dad was a professional golf coach and, yes sure, he got some of it from his dad. But Adam still had to consistently practise the right technique and actions in order to produce such an amazing-looking swing.

Tony Robbins says, 'It's not what we do once in a while that shapes our lives. It's what we do consistently.'

Do you understand where I am coming from here?

In order for you to produce results and go after your ultimate dream you will need to be perform certain tasks consistently to produce the results you desire. If you just do it now and then, that is not being consistent, and you will get a result here and there, but they will not be regular results and most likely you will be frustrated because your dream will still feel so far away.

When I have demonstrated a particular movement in the golf swing to people that I have taught, they would say, 'Well Tiff, that's alright for you, you make it look easy and I can't do that!' If only they had seen me when I first started playing golf; I was awkward and felt so uncomfortable, and played off the maximum handicap for women which is 45.

The reason I was able to achieve so much in golf so quickly was because I was willing to get a good coach, the right coach for me, and do the drills every day, be consistent with practice. Even when it got mundane, I still got out of bed every day and hit that driving range first thing in the morning, working on the drills to refine my skills. Yes, even when it was pouring with rain. It was called being consistent and diligent.

This applies in absolutely everything that you do, whether it is going after your dream, losing weight, working a job or studying a course. It's about showing up every day and doing the work. Some days when you don't feel like it, it can be a chore, it can be boring and sometimes it will take you longer to get the work done, just because it is mentally harder that day. Even if it does take longer to get the work done, it teaches you so much—how to be mentally tough, how to focus, to be disciplined in your actions and to stay in the present moment. There is so much that you can benefit from when things get harder, it teaches you to be tougher!

But what you have to understand is that it is the little consistent actions that you do each day that will give you the results.

A great book I read was *The Compound Effect* by Darren Hardy. Darren talks about the little actions that you do each day, that eventually compound after a period of time and bring you results. It will feel like the result appears out of the blue, but because you have been consistent each day, your actions have compounded and resulted in the reward.

When you are going after your big-ass dream, you have this big vision, you can see where you want to be, you can taste it! The reason you are just not there yet is because you haven't done what needs to be done to get there.

When golfers say to me, 'Tiff, you make it look so easy!' I say, 'Yes of course I do because I have done the work.' I drilled away for hours and hours every day working on my swing and all my shots to ensure that they would hold up in a tournament. I did the work on my mental game on a daily basis to ensure that when the pressure was on, I could rise to the challenge, stay focused, limit the distractions and just get on with it.

That's what it takes in sport, that's what it takes with everything.

What about weight? I hate to say it, but we are living in a world where people are getting larger and larger. In Australia, at the time of writing this book, our overweight percentages are something like sixty per cent for adults, with obesity having risen by about eighty per cent in the last thirty-three years. What about the kids? About twenty-five per cent of kids are overweight and we are considered to be the thirteenth fattest nation in the world. Interesting statistics considering that we pride ourselves on being a sporting nation.

These statistics frighten me for lots of reasons, however if you look at it from a consistency angle, we have this epidemic for one simple reason. We are consistently eating the wrong food, and a lot of the wrong food doesn't benefit our bodies. Hence we are getting fatter. This is called the Compound Effect.

The Compound Effect orks in two ways, a positive ripple effect and a negative ripple effect. Again we will look at weight as it is easy to explain and understand.

## THE NEGATiVE EFFECT

If you are consistently eating high-calorie foods, high-fat foods, highly processed foods and large portions of food, you are going to put on weight. The only way you can keep it at bay is if you train your butt off, but you will have to burn an exorbitant amount of calories, about the same as you are eating. But realistically let's say you eat all of that food and you don't work it off at all. Over a period of time you will put on weight, getting fatter and fatter. All of a sudden you will discover that you don't fit into your clothes, your body is chubby and you don't know how you got there. But, if you look back at what you have done, it was eating fatty foods on a daily basis that has caused the weight gain.

Have you been consistent? Sure you have, but you have consistently done something that is negative and that will have a negative effect on you and your body.

## THE POSiTiVE EFFECT

You are consistently eating smaller portions of food, with all the right proteins, vegetables, carbohydrates and good fats. You limit the amount of high-fat food and high-calorie foods. You track your daily calorie intake and your daily calorie output. You work out at the gym or your sport and so on, but you are doing this consistently.

You will find over a period of time that you lose weight, you are stronger, healthier, fitter, more mentally alert and energized. You can perform better on a day-to-day basis simply because you look after yourself so much better.

◎

Which one would work for you?

Being consistent with looking after yourself so that you are more focused, alert and feeling good within or the one where you are whacking on the kilos feeling sluggish, tired and frustrated?

Consistency is just that—what you do on a regular basis to help you achieve what it is you want to achieve.

◎

Write out these questions in your journal and answer them.

1.  How consistent are you in pursuing your dream?

2.  Are you working on your dream every day?

3.  Are you working on the skills that need to be refined to ensure you achieve your dream?

4.  Do you have a plan in place of what you need to do to achieve your dream?

5.  Are there habits that will help you gain the consistency that you must have to achieve your dream?

6.  Are there systems you need to help you gain the consistency that you must have to achieve your dream?

If you don't have defined answers to these questions, do not be concerned as we will discover what you need to have in place with habits and systems. Plus the last chapter of this book is structured so that you can develop your plan to get to working on your ultimate dream.

## WHAT HABiTS DO WE NEED TO HAVE IN PLACE?

We have talked about consistency in this chapter. It is the consistent actions that you do on a daily basis that will be what give you the results.

Now this applies to the habits you are utilizing throughout the day. What are habits? Habits are routines of behaviour or automatic actions; you don't think about them, you just do them.

Smoking is a great example of a habit, isn't it? If you smoke every day what happens? You have smoky breath. Your fingers and fingernails go yellow. Your skin gets dry. You have to have a cigarette regularly throughout the day. You can't live without it.

What are the results of smoking? A bad chesty cough, stinky breath and smoking could lead to lung cancer and worse. But it is just a habit that has been formed, isn't it? It is a routine of behaviour that is done on a daily basis and gives you results from doing it.

What about someone who looks after their body?

Arnold Schwarzenegger is a prime example. He won the Mr Universe title five times and the Mr Olympia titles seven times. How was that achieved? His dedication to training, to looking after his body, eating the correct food that was going to give him strength, power, muscle and shred his body. It was the daily habits that he adopted that gave him the advantage over everyone else.

◎

What about you? What are your habits? Let's identify them below.

In your journal write the answers to these questions:

1. What time do I wake up in the morning?

2. How do I feel when I wake up in the morning?

3. What are the first five actions I take when I get out of bed?

4. Do I go to the gym or do some type of exercise in the morning?

5. What do I have for breakfast?

6. What is my attitude like in the morning when I think about what I have to do throughout the day?

7. Do I go to the gym or do some type of exercise throughout the day?

8. What is my attitude like at lunch time?

9. What do I have for lunch?

10. What do I eat for snacks throughout the day?

11. What is my attitude like mid afternoon?

12. What do I have for dinner?

13. What is my attitude like at night?

14. How do I feel and what thoughts run through my mind when I am getting ready for bed?

'Why so many questions Tiff?'

Well, we want to see if there are any patterns, or habits forming here. You may find that you are routine orientated, so more than you thought, in the way you behave and in the way that you think. This is what we want to identify to see if there are habits that you need to remove that are not benefiting you. Plus we also want to see the habits that *are* benefiting you.

After answering those questions, what have you noticed?

Are there some habits that are great that you would like to keep?

Are there some habits that no longer serve you and that you would like to replace with better habits?

In your journal write the answers to these questions:

1. What habits have you identified that are working for you?

2. What habits have you identified that are not working for you?

3. The habits that are working for you, why are they working so well?

4. The habits that are not working for you, why are they not working so well?

It's really important that you do the exercise above now. Don't wait until you have finished this chapter. I want to encourage you to do it now.

*With these habits that you have identified that are not serving you, what habits can you replace them with that will give you an advantage?*

## WHAT HABITS HAVE YOU FOUND THAT CAN WORK BETTER FOR YOU?

I will share the habits that really work for me—they may be the same as for you. These habits are simple and basic. But I find if you keep things simple and basic you are building good solid foundations. When you have good solid foundations you can build on them to grow and expand. Just like a house. When you have all of the foundations in place, you can then build the house on that solid structure. It won't falter. Even if the house itself breaks down, gets blown over in a hurricane, you can rebuild on the foundation because it is still in place. When things get tough you always go back to the foundations, the basics, and start again.

I am not saying that my habits are perfect and you should do them all my way. Just use them as a base to guide you. Some you may use and they will work for you, some you won't and you will find ones that you feel give you a better advantage. That's great. Whatever works for you will be the key as long as you are moving forward, growing and not standing still, waiting.

Habits that work for me are:

- ⊙ getting up early in the morning—4.00 a.m.

- ⊙ doing meditation early in the morning before a workout (keeps me focused and in the moment)

- ⊙ working in the gym—weight training, cardio or yoga

- ⊙ having a protein shake for breakfast

- ⊙ planning out my day

- ⊙ being disciplined to follow my plan for the day

- ⊙ eating healthy proteins, carbohydrates and good fats to give me energy and focus

- ⊙ drinking healthy drinks that keep me energized and focused

- ⊙ reading for at least thirty minutes per day (helps me learn and grow)

- ⊙ studying courses or studying successful people (helps me learn and grow)

- ⊙ going to bed early (ensures I have good sleep and am rested to approach the new day with energy, creativity and focus)

If you can identify the new habits you want and need to adopt, then start introducing them into your life today. Don't wait until you have finished this book, or you have worked on and done the plan outlined in the last chapter. Take action now and get on with it. Don't waste time anymore. The way to achieve your ultimate dreams is to take action and get the best out of you. You will be more motivated to finish this book so you can get out there and take on the world.

## HABiTS ARE IN PLACE BUT DO I NEED A SYSTEM FOR MY HABiTS?

I would say a big fat yes!

Habits are perfect to move you forward, but forming them into a system and making you more systemised is significant to achieving your ultimate dreams.

So what is a system?

A system can be defined as a set of principles or procedures according to which something is done or a method in which something is done.

I am a huge fan, actually, I just *love* systems. I believe that for anything you want to achieve, you must have a system in place or a method in place, as it will make you more efficient and get you the results that you want.

The way I learn anything, the way I teach anything, is all in a system.

When I was learning tennis growing up, I wasn't that clear on what it was that I needed to do to make each of the tennis strokes work. It was like someone put the racquet in my hand and said, 'Off you go.' To be honest, I don't really remember having any real technical lessons on how to do the shots. Don't get me wrong, I did have lessons, I went to weekly clinics and as a teenager I had many private lessons. But my memory of it was just hitting balls in rally situations, not really getting the finer points sorted out so I could really excel, the way I wanted to.

When I look back I was always a very frustrated kid. My parents always said I was a moody kid, a moody teenager—I got that one a lot! But I didn't think I was moody, I just felt frustrated because I wanted to get so much more out of my tennis but I didn't know what was missing. Sure, I shared with you my lack of belief and so on earlier in this book, but there was also a huge frustration hanging over me. This huge frustration was actually the lack of a system.

If we look around at anything we do, there is a method for doing things. There is a method for brushing your teeth, a method in which you drive the car, a method to how you walk—it's everywhere you look if you really think about it.

In order for you to achieve your ultimate dream, you must have systems in place that will be part of your plan to accomplish your goals and dreams.

I learned about systems in two ways.

The first was from my biomechanics lecturer at university. It was the way he taught. I talked about it in chapter on learning the skills. We were learning volleyball and the way he taught was to brake down everything into little chunks. Once we got those little chunks in place for each of the skills in the volleyball strokes, we could piece those little chunks back together and form a complete technical shot. We could then use that skill to apply to a game.

The second was in me teaching others. When I started teaching tennis I was still at university, I was about twenty-three years old, and that wonderful insight into volleyball learning came later. When I started teaching, I didn't have a system in place for how to teach tennis. I would just rock up and do the lessons. Why? I didn't know how to teach, I just winged it!

Not a good move but it taught me a lot about systems.

My first tennis lesson was with a group of teenagers. Mmmm how hard could that be? I loved tennis, so I just assumed everyone who came for tennis lessons would feel the same as me. Well, to my shock, they didn't feel as excited about tennis as I did.

I thought all I would have to do was feed tennis balls to these teenagers; they could practise their strokes, take it in turns, play some games of tennis at the end and everything would be wonderful. That's what I did growing up, but what I discovered was that, because I wanted to be there, I was a coach's dream: I just wanted to learn and play tennis.

I received a huge and really fast lesson that day about lack of structure and lack of systems. The teenagers did what all kids do with lack of structure. They mucked around and balls were flying from one side of the court to the other. The teenagers were trying to hit each other with the balls, screaming at each other and I kept ducking for cover so I didn't get hit. I was screaming at these teenagers and their parents were screaming at me.

It was a lesson I have never forgotten.

But after the wonderful insight I received from my university lecturer, about how to systemize a technique and how to structure lessons, no other tennis lesson was the same as that first one ever again.

I applied all of these systems and structures to my future lessons in tennis, to starting my sports-skills business, to learning golf and later to teaching golf. Even in writing this book I have put in place a certain system to ensure you benefit from each of these chapters.

The point of the stories in this section is for you to understand that it's crucial to have a system in place for learning and developing your dream. The best way to learn your system is to then teach it to others.

This is where teaching golf, more than any other sport, has had a huge impact for me. Golf is such a precision sport. Technically you want to be in the right position in each of your shots at the right time to get the best out of your shots. When I learned to play, it was about chunking it down and developing a system in which I could hit the ball consistently and get the results I was after on the golf course in tournaments. When I moved into teaching the game, I needed to develop a simple, easy-to-learn system that anyone at any age could use to learn the golf techniques. And yes, the older generation could learn just as well as the younger generation. The golf system I developed worked for all ages.

I have systems in place for everything I do, to ensure I get the maximum that I can out of me each day. No, it is not like being a robot. It's called working smarter not harder. I used to think I wasn't working hard enough, and that's why I wasn't achieving what I wanted. The problem was my lack of systems in place. I was working harder doing the same things over and over again expecting a different result. That wasn't the answer. The answer was analysing what was not working and what I should improve and implement in order to work more effectively and efficiently.

◎

For whatever you are pursuing, we need to recognize that you do or don't have systems in place.

In your journal write the answers to these questions:

1. Do I have a morning system for how to set myself up for a successful and productive day?

2. Do I have a system in place for working on my mental skills?

3. Do I have a system in place for working on my physical skills?

4. Do I have a system in place for training my body?

5.  Do I have a system in place for eating the right food?

6.  Do I have a system in place for learning and growing my mind?

7.  Do I have a system in place for learning skills?

8.  Do I have a system in place for evaluating my day?

9.  Do I have a system in place for planning out my day?

10. Do I have a system in place for planning out my week?

11. Do I have a system in place for planning out each quarter of the year?

12. Do I have a system in place for planning out my year?

13. Do I have a system in place for evaluating my week?

14. Do I have a system in place for evaluating each quarter of the year?

15. Do I have a system in place for evaluating my year?

These questions are designed to trigger you to identify that you will need systems in place if you are going to go after that ultimate dream.

So how did you go with these? Did you become more aware of the lack of systems in place, or were you more aware that you have some systems in place already?

If you answered 'no' more than three times, then it is time to get some systems in place. Remember it will be the daily actions you have in place that will compound over time to give you the results that you want. Consequently, you will need systems in place to do that.

Let's develop a simple system now so that you can apply it to each area of your life. A huge point I want to stress with you here is that you will need systems in place in each area of your life. This is because all of the areas will contribute to the success of your dream.

For example, if you are pursuing a sporting career, you will not only have to have a learning system in place for learning and refining your skills, but you will also require a system in place for working on your mindset, a system in place for training your body, a system in place for eating the right food to maximize your mind and body, and a system in place for relaxation and down time. I think you get my point.

Here we will develop a system for you that you can apply to each area of your life. I will pose questions below for you to answer to develop your system, then you can pose these same questions towards each area of your life that will require a system for you to achieve your ultimate dream.

## DEVELOP A SiMPLE SYSTEM YOU CAN USE

Think about the skill that you want to improve. The one that is of utmost importance for you. When you are ready get out your journal answer the following questions in relation to the skill you want to improve. In the examples in these questions I have used a golf swing to assist you in identifying how you can develop your system to improve your skills.

1.  What is the skill I want to improve? E.g. a skill, such as a golf swing.

2.  What do I need to improve in this skill? For example, you are struggling for consistency with your golf swing.

3.  What are the problem areas in this skill? For example, work with your coach, take a video of your golf swing and identify the problem areas in your golf swing.

4.  What are the actions I will need to take to improve each step of this skill? For example, work on drills given to you by your coach.

5.  What is the result or feedback I will require from these actions to ensure the skill has improved? For example, are you able to do the drills with success or are you still struggling with the drills?

6.  When the skill has attained the level required, what must I do? For example, keep continuing to practice the drills.

This is a simple system that you can use to get yourself started. Over time you will discover that it will require refinement, but once you have a foundational system in place, you can continue to work on improving your system.

# CHAPTER 9

# MENTAL FOCUS AND CONTROLLiNG YOUR EMOTiONS

*'Any active sportsman has to be very focused; you've got to be in the right frame of mind. If your energy is diverted in various directions, you do not achieve the results. I need to know when to switch on and switch off: and the rest of the things happen around that. Cricket is in the foreground, the rest is in the background.' – Sachin Tendulkar*

Absolutely anything you do in your life, whether it be sport, school, study, business, training, learning a skill and everything else will require you to be mentally switched on and mentally focused, as well as being able to control your emotions around your mental focus.

What is being mentally focused?

My definition of being mentally focused is staying in the moment and working on a specific task with one-hundred-percent-attention. Anything and everything that you work on requires one hundred per cent attention.

There is a myth out there that women can multi-task. Of course we can juggle a few things at once, but if you look at it, how effective are we really when we are

doing a few things at once? I used to pride myself on multi-tasking: how good am I when I can get this, this and that done, not a problem! But what I found was that I was just half doing everything and not fully completing anything.

My husband and I have a running joke that men can only do one thing at a time, and my husband is very much like that. One-thing-at-a-time man! However the older and more aware I become I am finding that he is spot on. He will love me admitting this, so here I am admitting it! One thing at a time is more effective than attempting to be a multi-tasker.

If you don't agree with me, then I will pose an exercise for you to try out.

In your journal do these exercises below. You will need a timer.

## EXERCISE 1: MULTI-TASKING

1. When you are ready I want you to have two columns. One will be for the alphabet and the other will be for numbers.

2. Set your timer because you will be recording how long it will take you to complete this exercise.

3. Write the letter A in the first column and in the second column write the number 1.

4. Then repeat with the letter B in the first column and the number 2 in the second column.

5. Keep repeating this until you have completed the letter Z and number 26.

6. Record your time for this whole exercise.

## EXERCiSE 2: ONE THiNG AT A TiME

1. When you are ready I want you to have two columns. One will be for the alphabet and the other will be for numbers.

2. Set your timer because you will be recording how long it will take you to complete this exercise.

3. Write the letter A in the first column, followed by the letter B underneath A, then the letter C underneath B and so on in that one column until you have got to the letter Z.

4. Then move straight into the second column and right the number 1, then under the number 1 write the number 2, then under the number 2 write the number 3 and so on until you get to the number 26.

5. Record your time for this whole exercise.

OK are you done?

I really want you to do both of these exercises before you read on because then you will understand even more what I am talking about when I am emphasizing the importance of mental focus.

I am going to assume that you have done both of these exercises. What result did you have?

Did you find that Exercise 2—One Thing At A Time - resulted in a shorter time?

If you said, 'Yes Tiff, it was faster!' then welcome to the discovery of the importance of mental focus and doing one thing at a time. If you found that you did Exercise 1 quicker, then you are so much more advanced than me and congratulations. I haven't yet heard of anyone being quicker for Exercise 1, so if you were, please let me know.

I am going to assume you did the same as me and that you found that Exercise 2 was much quicker. When I first did that exercise it blew me away with amazement simply because I always believed that I was such a great multi-tasker. I always seemed to be just so busy, but never got anything finished. When I did both those exercises I found that I should only focus on one thing at a time and get it done before starting the next task.

When I became aware that I was more efficient and effective through the process of doing one thing at a time, it completely changed my awareness, focus and attention to the details.

What I notice now with people around me is the lack of attention to detail, the lack of focus and the lack of patience. Very interesting. I believe that the universe sends me these people to slow them down and help them to really focus on what they want to achieve and how they are going to achieve that. These people I work with always comment on how patient I am with them. But I get it, I too was impatient, I too had a lack of focus and I too had a lack of attention to details.

If I go back to my tennis days as a junior competing in tournaments and wanting to break into the professional tennis circuit I can see there was a huge lack of attention to detail, plus the lack of focus and the lack of patience was also there.

I was trying so hard to do everything. I trained really hard, I did extra training so I could be fitter and last longer in matches, and be quicker running down all of those shots that I would have to retrieve and play back over the net. I didn't really have a plan for training, I just did extra of what I had learned: just did more long-distance running to build up my stamina and more sprints to make me quicker around the court.

Earlier in this book I also talked about my lack of focus. I couldn't focus mentally on what I had to do on the court to stay in the game and win matches. Mum would often make a comment about me 'going walkabout'. It wasn't that I walked off, it was that I couldn't maintain focus on the tennis court because I had no mental strategies. I couldn't control my emotions, and I worried about losing and what people on the sidelines thought of me.

You can see how this would all compound and then how my lack of patience would appear. I wouldn't hang in there and grind it out, I wasn't patient with learning and developing myself into a better player and even when I gave up at the age of twenty. I wasn't patient enough to give myself more time to work it all out. I believed if I hadn't made it by twenty then it was over. What a massive mistake that was! Only twenty years old and already giving up! If only I had my time over again with the knowledge I now possess.

This is why I continue to share stories with you, because I don't want you to give up on you. This is why I share what is required to take yourself to the heights and the level you want to go to.

It was interesting, however, when I took up golf. I didn't have that lack of attention to detail, the lack of focus nor the lack of patience. It was all there in force. I put that down to experience and the shift in my mental approach.

Since my early twenties to the point when I took up golf at thirty-four, I had been on a huge learning curve. I had learned how to break down skills into small compartments and I had learned how to communicate in an easy and understandable way to teach kids, teenagers and adults. I had developed teaching systems and strategies plus, the big one, I had learned the art of patience. All of this is relevant to having mental focus and controlling your emotions.

If you ever want to learn how to be more detailed, have more focus and be patient, I suggest that you either learn to play golf or learn an instrument. You will learn so much about you, and then imparting that knowledge, such as through teaching golf or the instrument to someone else: that will teach you patience.

When I have taught golf to adults, especially, I can pretty much tell each student's personality type in one lesson. I can tell if they are a big-picture person, an attention-to-detail person, their level of patience, and whether they can maintain their focus.

When you are learning golf it will require you to focus. It will require you to be aware of the detail and to be able to repeat the actions over and over again. It will require you to stay in the moment and focus only on one thing at a time. It will require you to control your emotions, not get frustrated, angry or upset and it will require you to be patient.

That's what I noticed when I was learning golf. I understood so much more learning this sport because the experience I had already acquired through teaching benefitted me in the learning process and everything else that went with it.

What golf teaches you is that it will require one hundred per cent of your attention, whether you are learning a skill for the first time or you are a seasoned professional. If you want to perform at any level, you will need to stay in the moment of that shot, which means your mind will be clear and you will feel in a 'flow state' or 'in a zone' when you are playing the shot. Nothing else will enter your mind.

It is interesting when you watch a professional golfer play as you will assume that they have got it all together because their skill level is so high and they make it look so easy. But what you don't see is what is going on in their mind, the level of mental commitment they have to make in order for them to perform at their best.

You will hear in interviews with professional athletes that they say, 'I just couldn't find my swing today' or 'I couldn't do anything wrong. It all just happened, it was awesome.' This is all to do with their mental state, how they control their emotions during their performance and how patient they are when working through the mental challenges that they will face in their tournaments and games.

What I discovered when I learned how to play golf was how to stay in the moment, how to control my emotions during learning and competing, plus the level of patience I needed to apply in order to achieve my golf goals.

The biggest breakthrough I had in competing on the golf course was definitely learning to stay in the moment and giving one-hundred-per-cent focus to a shot. In the beginning of competing in golf I would constantly not trust my shots, expect mistakes, and not give one-hundred-per-cent focus to the shots because I would be expecting to make a mistake! I lacked self-trust and doubted my abilities because the sport was new to me and my tennis demons were still buzzing around in my head. If I made a mistake I would say, 'Told you! I knew you would stuff it up!' If you think about that comment you could say I was actually focusing on stuffing up the shot and making a mistake, rather than making the shot.

That's not what I wanted to do, but I would make mistakes because for so many years I had programmed my mind to be negative about my results. It surprises me that I achieved so much in sport in my earlier years with this poor mental attitude and my poor focus.

Anyway, back to the story!

My breakthrough came when I was standing over the ball about to play a shot, a full golf-swing shot, to hit the ball to land on the green. I said to myself, 'Tiff, what if you trusted your shot, gave one-hundred-per-cent focus, all of the focus you could give it, and if you made a mistake then it's OK, you can learn from it?' I then said, 'OK, I will do that because it's not working the other way!'

That Aha Moment, the Awakening, the Awareness, the Breakthrough or whatever you would like to call it, was the biggest breakthrough that I had ever had with anything. I was learning to trust my decisions, I was learning to stay in the moment and completely give one hundred per cent of my mental energy in that moment to playing that shot.

Amazing!

I realized then that I was spending too much time in the past. I would drift into the future every now and then, but very rarely would I stay in the present moment. This is now what I constantly teach whether it be in sport, in business or in life: be in the moment and give the best effort in that moment that you can. Give the one-hundred-per-cent focus right now. Don't think about the past, don't think about the future, just stay here, right now in what you are doing. I am not saying don't plan for the future, of course you want to do that, and learn from your past, but all you can control right now is what you do in this moment.

That is the power of mental focus!

◎

*Where do you spend most of your time in your mind—the past, the future or the present?*

You can't control what happened in the past, because it is long gone, the past is the past. But you can control what happens in the future by what you are controlling in the present.

In your journal, write out your answers to these questions:

1. Where do you spend most of your time in your mind—the past, the future or the present?

2. If you have identified that you spend more time in the past, why? What is it about the past that causes you to spend your mental energy there?

3. If you have identified that you spend more time in the future, why? What is it about the future that causes you to spend your mental energy there?

4. If you have identified that you spend more time in the present, why? What is it about the present that causes you to spend your mental energy there?

What have you discovered about you?

You have discovered where you are spending most of your mental energy, correct? Do not worry if you are spending more time in the past or more time in the future than in the present moment. All we wanted to do here was help you to become more aware of where your mental focus is right now. If we need to tweak the focus then we can.

Always, always, always we're creating an awareness of what is going on for you. Once we know where your awareness is then we can put action steps in place to ensure we are working on you achieving your ultimate dreams and not being held back.

## HOW CAN YOU GAIN MORE FOCUS?

This is a great question. How can you gain more focus?

Have you ever heard people say, 'I need to concentrate more', 'I need to focus more' and get really annoyed with themselves when they don't focus or concentrate? Do you know why they don't focus or concentrate more? Because they don't know how!

Over the years teaching a few thousand kids, I often heard parents yell out to their kids, 'Billy, just focus!' Or at sports games with soccer parents, 'Come on Evie, focus!'

Even the golfers I have taught over the years get really angry with themselves, because they have poor concentration, and when they make a mistake in their shot and it doesn't work, they put themselves down, tell themselves what an idiot they are. They yell at themselves 'to focus', but they make the same sort of mistakes repeatedly. They repeat the same pattern endlessly: mistakes are made, they put themselves down, they yell at themselves. They do the same thing over and over again expecting a different result. You have to change what you are doing to get a different result.

There is a very simple technique that you can use to assist you in gaining more focus. I use it on a daily basis. It has helped me improve every single task I work on.

It helps me train better in the gym. It helps me perform my yoga practice better. It helps me focus better on the golf course or tennis court. It helps me focus better on anything that I put my efforts towards.

This simple technique is a breathing technique; a very simple form of meditation.

Right throughout this book I have emphasized keeping everything simple and getting the foundations in place. Again, this is another foundation for you to set up to be part of your success formula that will get you to achieving your ultimate dream!

## BOX BREATHING MEDITATION

Box breathing meditation is a very simple breathing technique. It is called box breathing because you are breathing in for a period of seconds, holding your breath for a period of seconds, breathing out for a period of seconds and holding out that breath for a period of seconds. It is also know an four-square breathing. This breathing technique is benefical for those who want to meditate and/or reduce stress.

Here is an example how box breathing works. You breathe in for five seconds, you hold your breath for five seconds, you breathe out for five seconds and you hold for five seconds.

Sounds quite simple, right?

Do you know how many people I have introduced to this breathing exercise? I cannot tell you an exact number—lots!—but what I will tell you is that very few of them apply this technique.

I always suggest doing it for five minutes. The comeback comment I receive from this suggestion is that, 'I can't sit still for five minutes! My mind won't stop!'

Do you know why these people can't sit still for five minutes or why their minds won't stop? Because they haven't trained themselves to do it. Meditation is a skill just like any sports skill and you have to learn how to do it. And by the way, your mind won't stop, thoughts will pop in and out, but it's all about how you control those thoughts.

I am as active as anyone. I grew up as a sportsperson and I hated to feel as though I were trapped at school having to sit down in a chair. I love moving around, I love that feeling of freedom, but I will say this: it will be the best five minutes a day in your life; it will be five minutes that you totally devote to you.

The best time to do the box breathing meditation is in the morning when you get out of bed. I recommend doing it then because everything else seems to get in the way once you get going, and for one reason or another you just won't make it a priority in your day. Best to get it done first, then it is done.

## THE BOX BREATHiNG MEDiTATiON TECHNiQUE

Below is a simple system to follow to perform your daily meditation. Just follow the steps.

1. Pick a quiet place in your home.

2. Sit in a chair.

3. Set your timer on your phone for five minutes (put your phone on aeroplane mode, we don't want any disruptions).

4. Breathe in for five seconds (count it in your mind as you breath in 1-2-3-4-5)

5. Hold your breath for five seconds (count it in your mind as you hold your breath 1-2-3-4-5)

6. Breath out for five seconds (count it in your mind as you breath out 1-2-3-4-5)

7.  Hold your breath for five seconds (count it in your mind as you hold your breath 1-2-3-4-5)

8.  Keep breathing in this format until your timer buzzes.

I challenge you to try this now. You can keep reading once you have done it as there are some questions I want to ask you once you have done it. But for now, just stop reading, set your phone to aeroplane mode, set the timer for five minutes and test it out. Don't wait and say I'll do it later, because later never comes. *Do it now!*

◎

I will assume that you have done the box breathing meditation for five minutes. See if you can answer these questions as if we were just having a chat over a coffee.

⊙  Was there anything that stood out for you?

⊙  Was there anything that you became more aware of?

⊙  Did five minutes seem like a really long time?

⊙  Did you find that you were checking the timer because it was taking so long?

⊙  Did you check the timer to see if you even set the timer, because you couldn't remember if you set it?

⊙  Did you find that you drifted in and out of counting?

⊙  Were you finding that you had a lot of thoughts popping in and out of your head that were distracting you from counting and breathing?

I am going to predict that you said that you were distracted as you had so many thoughts, ideas, things you must do today popping in and out of your head. You most likely found that you lost track of counting and your breathing, you easily got side-tracked with your thoughts, plus you kept checking the timer because it took so long to finish.

Congratulations, you have now become more aware of how your mental focus operates.

Can it be improved?

Of course it can, but you have got to want it to improve. You have got to want to gain better mental focus because if you do, wow, watch what happens to you then!

When I discovered this simple technique—I can't remember exactly where I was, a conference perhaps—I thought I would just try it but do it consistently for a month to see if it would have any impact.

Guess what? It sure did! It had a *huge* impact and I still do it every day and I have found that it's not the amount of time that you dedicate to meditation, it is the quality of meditation that you apply.

You will find if you do meditate (perform this breathing technique) for a period of time, say a month, that you will start to shift your mental state into a flow and tend to stay in the moment more and be able to focus just on your breathing. It will take practise to get there but it can happen.

What I noticed early on through this simple daily five-minute meditation was:

⊙  I became more aware of my thoughts,

⊙  I was more aware of being distracted by my thoughts,

⊙  I was more aware of drifting into the past and the future with my thoughts,

⊙ I was more aware that I didn't spend much time in the present moment, and

⊙ I was able to let go of my thoughts and just go back to focusing on counting.

We experience a lack of focus constantly in our sport, our studying, our schooling, our training, work and everything that we do. Just imagine if you could focus better just by doing a simple meditation technique for five minutes a day?

Would you be able to get more done?

Would you focus on the task or skills that required your attention?

Would you be less distracted and focus more on your ultimate dream?

I challenge you to try it. But, not just once! You must do it for thirty days in a row.

*My challenge to you: Five-minute meditation for thirty days.*

## CONTROLLiNG YOUR EMOTiONS

You can control your emotions to get the best effort out of you that you can in a focused, achievable way, and not allow your emotions to take over and control you, to spiral you out of control.

Remember I shared with you the time when I played a tennis tournament against a well-known Australian tennis player on the tour and I got absolutely smashed 6–0 6–0? My concerns and focus all the thoughts running through my mind were about what everyone on the sideline thought of me, that I was letting myself down and that I looked like an idiot. Then I cried uncontrollably after losing. Well, that was not being able to control my emotions.

I had no mental strategies in place for how to deal with performance anxiety, no strategies in place if my body froze up and couldn't move, and no strategies in place to focus on playing one shot at a time or to stop myself from becoming angry, frustrated and crying my eyes out after the defeat.

◎

Have you ever felt this way? Are you feeling like this today?

In your journal, write the answers to these questions:

1. What was the biggest moment, the one that stands out for you most, where you lost control of your emotions and it had a negative effect?

2. What happened at that time?

3. What type of emotions were running through your body?

4. What were you thinking?

5. Why do you believe you were thinking those thoughts?

6. What are you more aware of right now answering these questions above?

◎

It's tough to teach yourself how to control your emotions. It's not something that you can just do by waving a magic wand over your head and 'hey presto' you are now in control of your emotions. It will require effort and reframing your mind. It will require you to get to the root cause of the problem then reprogram your mind in how you want to be: in control of your emotions and the type of behaviour you display. Not for the world to see, but for you. It's about creating a set of principles, standards and values that you live by and by which you expect yourself to operate.

This decision—deciding to get to the root cause of your difficulties with emotional control—will be yours to make. As will creating a set of standards and values for yourself. I suggest you need to make that decision, but I will leave that in your court. I can only guide you and suggest you take action but, at the end of the day the decision will be yours.

Once you make that decision, something amazing will happen. You will feel a sense of urgency, a sense of energy, a sense of alertness and a remarkable sense of focus.

It is amazing when this shift occurs. It's there inside of you, waiting to be released. Trust me it is, but you need to be the one who releases it and lets it come alive in you. When it does, an incredible sense of focus will shift you into being a powerhouse of creativity and production.

I just love that feeling! I'm addicted to feeling this way, like an adrenalin junkie who loves to jump off mountains and paraglide their way down to the bottom. I want you to be addicted to it too!

## ESTABLISHING YOUR SET OF STANDARDS AND VALUES

What are standards?

My definition of standards is the way in which you expect yourself to operate at a particular level.

For example, your standard of living includes you expecting to make your bed every morning and brush your teeth after breakfast before you leave the house; that you meditate every morning as soon as you get out of bed to help keep yourself focused throughout the day. That's a simple example but one which is easy for you to relate to.

What are values?

My definition of values is that they are your core beliefs; a code by which you stand. An example of one of your core beliefs could be that you believe in respect. Respect to you could mean that you respect each person you speak to and have respect for all humanity, or that you do not judge people and have respect for their opinions even if you don't agree with them.

It's time to set your standards, the level at which you will operate on a daily basis, what you will expect from yourself.

In your journal, answer this question:

*What are my standards, my daily modes of operation?*

If you get stuck for ideas, I will list some below. They are mine. What you will notice too, over time, is that your standards will evolve and change. Mine do and yours will also.

## MY STANDARDS

- ⊙ I wake up every morning at 4 a.m. to prepare for the day.

- ⊙ I go to bed every evening at 8 p.m. to listen to hypnosis audio and give myself restful sleep.

- ⊙ I do my morning miracles every morning to prepare my mind for the day.

- ⊙ I meditate every morning.

- ⊙ I ask this question each day and answer it: How do I generate the income I desire?

- ⊙ I have a protein shake every morning to start my day with power and focus.

- ⊙ I eat protein, veggies and fruit throughout the day to keep my energy levels high.

- ⊙ I do a cleanse day at least once per week.

- ⊙ I plan out my day every day.

- ⊙ I don't finish my work day until I have achieved my set tasks.

- ⊙ I work on my goals every day.

- ⊙ I work on my goals because my tribe needs me to be my best.

- ⊙ I accomplish my goals because my tribe needs me to achieve my goals.

- ⊙ I read every day for thirty minutes.

- ⊙ I apply what I read that will benefit me and my tribe.

- ⊙ I ask myself this question at end of each day: How can I be better?

There are a few more to add to this list but I think you get the point I am making here. As you can see, these standards are those by which I expect myself to operate. What I have become more aware of since developing my standards over the past few years is the lack of standards other people have for themselves.

It is really fascinating that people won't have a list of standards for themselves yet they will expect others to have particular standards, whether this is conscious or subconscious, and then criticize others for not having the same non-existent so-called standards they have. Have you observed how people around you tend to just go through the motions? They just want to get the day out of the way. That's it. There is no purpose or structure to their day, they just go to work etc. because they have to. Just imagine if they had a set of standards set up for themselves: they could get more done in the day, enjoy being alive, be more productive and even have a great time at work. They may even want to advance in their work. Wouldn't that be fantastic!

When you lay out your list of standards on paper, you can always have them in plain sight and it gives you a visual reminder of what to expect from yourself. When you set a level of standards for youself, you will become more aware of your expectations and when you don't live up to your standards, you will be quick to remind yourself how you need to operate.

Having standards written down not only reminds you of what you expect from yourself, but it is also a prompt to remember to read them out loud to constantly reinforce your level of standards.

◎

Once you have written out your standards, read them out loud and really listen to them.

The more you instil these in your mind, the more you will have the intention to live by the level of standards you set for yourself.

◎

Our next step is to establish your core values, your core set of beliefs.

In your journal answer this question:

*What are my values, my core set of beliefs?*

If you are stuck for where to start to establish your core set of values, here is an example of mine below. Some may resonate with you so go ahead and use them. These are meant to trigger you, so that you can establish your own set of values.

## TiFF'S CORE VALUES

*Respect—I respect every person I speak with and have respect for all humanity.*

*No judgement—I do not judge people, I respect their opinions even if different from mine.*

*Leadership—I lead people to achieve their goals and I lead by example.*

*Adventure—I create adventure in my life.*

*Energy—I have the energy to train, focus and work hard to achieve my goals, and for my family and tribe.*

*Example—I set an example to younger girls, teenage girls and women to strive to be their best.*

*Strive—I strive to be on my A-game every day and to give my best effort every day.*

*Meditate—I meditate each day because it keeps me focused and in the moment.*

*Focus—I focus on every task because it helps me achieve my goals for me, my family and my tribe.*

*Love—I love everyone, everyone deserves to be loved.*

*Care—I care for everyone.*

*Relationships—I love my husband and my family more than anything. I spend quality time with my family.*

When you lay out your list of values on paper, you have them in plain sight: it gives you a visual reminder of them. When you create your values, you will become more aware of what they are, and when you live by these values you are quick to remind yourself of them and how you expect yourself to operate around them.

Having a written list of values in front of you not only reminds you of what you expect from yourself, but it can also be used as a prompt to read them out loud, constantly reinforcing your core beliefs, your core values.

Once you have written out your values, then read them out loud and really listen to them. The more you instil these in your mind, the more you will have the intention to live by the values you set for yourself.

# SETTING UP A SIMPLE SYSTEM TO CONTROL YOUR EMOTIONS

We have established your standards and values, which will set up in your mind your expectations for yourself. But it won't be the answer to controlling your emotions. It will, however, establish within your mind an awareness, most likely more awareness than you have ever had, of how you react to certain situations and those reactions that you would like to improve on.

Usually when we react to something emotionally, the reaction is caused by an event that has happened in the past. You create a story out of that event, your emotions get involved, you get upset, angry or happy (it doesn't have to be a negative emotion), then there is a result. *Event + Emotional Reaction + Story = Result.*

Think about a big moment that has happened in your life. What transpired? Something happened, you reacted to it, created a whole story around it and applied a meaning to it. And a combination of all of that has given you either a negative or positive outcome.

Let's go back to my tennis career and that woeful match I have relived with you numerous times throughout this book. Now I have said 'woeful'. That's because I created a reaction to that event. If you look at it, I played a match and I lost the match—that's it!

But in my mind, I played a tennis match, I got angry, frustrated, felt humiliated and then I cried. From that I created this story that I was hopeless, a loser and I shouldn't be playing tennis because I was such a bad tennis player. I was worried and stressed about the people on the sideline watching me. I then lost the match, ran behind the clubhouse and cried my eyes out.

All it was, in the end, was a huge reaction to an event that happened in my life. The reason I can remember it so clearly is because I attached so much emotion to the event.

Just before, I asked you to go back into your past and identify a big moment that stood out to you in your life. I bet if we revisit that event right now, there will be a huge amount of emotion attached to that event. Would I be correct in asking that?

There is nothing wrong with attaching emotions to events, it just depends on how you ideally want to respond to an event like that in the future. Would you like to respond the same way or would you prefer a better approach that is more beneficial to you?

In sport there is a simple strategy to use when you make an error in the execution of a skill, or when the stroke or shot doesn't come off the way you would like it to.

This simple strategy is below:

1. Acknowledge you have made an error.

2. Acknowledge that you feel an emotion around the error.

3. Use a breathing technique to control emotion—change the emotional state.

4. Identify what the error was.

5. Identify how to correct the error.

6. Have a plan in mind for how to execute the shot more effectively next time.

◎

Now let's put together a simple strategy for you to control your emotions when you feel like you are going to lose it, and let your emotional state take control of you.

In your journal, write down these questions and answer them:

1.  What was the reaction?

2.  What were the emotions?

3.  What did you feel like doing?

4.  What was the result of that event that happened to you?

Now we are going to reframe it and change the way you respond.

Think again of that event that happened where you had that negative reaction, and use the steps below to change your way of looking at it.

## FiVE-STEP STRATEGY TO CONTROL YOUR EMOTiONS

1.  Acknowledge that you feel a negative emotion.

2.  Change the negative emotion—use a breathing technique. (How will you breathe to control the negative emotion?)

3.  Once you have given yourself time to settle, what is the ideal emotional response you would like to have?

4.  Where will you now dedicate your focus?

5.  What will be your ideal result from this event in a positive form?

This is just a simple plan we are putting into place for you, so that rather than reacting the way you usually would (and most likely you have been reacting this way for a long time, possibly since you were a child), we can reprogram the way you react or, in other words, how you respond. It will take some practice, because you have to remember you have been reacting a particular way for years, so it will take you time to work through it. But the important thing is that you now have a simple five-step strategy to control your emotions.

The best way to implement this strategy is to write it out first, then to talk about it with someone close to you, sharing with them what you are doing to change your focus and gain better control. Visualize it, see yourself actually laying out the written plan: You are under that pressure to react, but because you have your plan in place, because you have been mentally rehearsing it, you have shared and spoken about it, you are better equipped to deal with it.

## CHAPTER 10

# MANAGiNG YOURSELF AND YOUR ENERGY

*'It's so important to realize that every time you get upset, it drains your emotional energy. Losing your cool makes you tired. Getting angry a lot messes with your health.' – Joyce Meyer*

I feel this is a very important chapter for you because when you are chasing your ultimate dream, you tend to neglect everything else around you. It can affect your relationships, your health, your emotions, your fitness, your levels of energy and your mental state. You may be thinking, 'Tiff, I've got this covered, I am just going to work my butt off until I get my dream!'

You know what? I get it! I understand how badly you want to get on with it, you have a sense that it needs to be done and accomplished yesterday, you have that sense of urgency to get that dream happening and you can no longer waste any more time.

However, you will need to understand that if you do not: manage yourself properly; give yourself rest periods; spend time with loved ones; look after yourself in the sense of eating right, keeping your mind calm, ensuring you have good fitness levels and being enthused and motivated; nor stick to your set plan or schedule you will most likely hit burnout.

There is nothing worse than burnout. Believe me I know. I have experienced burnout many times in the past for all those reasons I laid out above. Because of my level of urgency to get my goals achieved, I have failed in the past to plan out my days, my weeks, my months and even the year. My personal relationships have been affected, by me not giving time to those who I have loved most. My energy tank has run on empty many times, and when this happens, everything and everyone around me suffers.

I neglect everyone and everything. I don't spend time on my goals and I don't work as effectively on my business or my sports. I don't spend time with my family or my husband and I don't eat as well as I normally do. I stop working out at the gym and I stop studying, learning and reading to expand my knowledge simply because I don't have anything left in the tank.

When there is nothing left in the tank, that is, when I have no energy, I have this feeling of a dark cloud hanging over my head. I am foggy, disillusioned and I feel very down within (some people may call it depression, I don't). I feel as though I have lost my way, I watch mindless programs on television at night and I go into survival mode just trying to get through the day. I end up going through the motions, just hanging in there to finish off the day.

This has happened many times over the years.

You may relate to this. How I operate is that I totally absorb myself in my goals: they are just everything to me. I work long hours on them, I have late nights and early mornings and plough through the day. It becomes obsessive. Don't get me wrong, I believe you must be obsessed about your goals, but not to the point that you are hitting burnout every six weeks!

And that was what was happening: every six weeks I was hitting burnout. I would often say to myself, 'Watch out, Tiff, you are going to hit burnout again!' In that moment, I would have a comeback and say, 'She'll be right!' But, the problem was I wasn't right. I was always burning out.

I am an all or nothing person!

I either give everything I have to that goal I want to accomplish or I just don't give it the time of day. It's never half-arsed! It's all or nothing!

I believe it's awesome to have this attitude because if you want to attain those big-ass goals you have to give all you have, but in a structured and managed way, so that you don't hit burnout. How we do that will be detailed in the next chapter in our plan, but I want you to be aware of it now so that you can identify how you are going to manage yourself so that you don't run out of puff!

There is nothing worse than burnout, as I have explained earlier. The problem with burnout is that you waste so much time in that space of survival mode. Nothing gets done because your energy levels have been depleted. You can't think clearly and every day appears to be a struggle and you can't understand why you are so exhausted.

When I have experienced burnout, it would take me up to three weeks to get back up on my feet. Three weeks is a lot of wasted time when you want to get those goals achieved. But the dilemma is that you can't get moving on them, because there is psychological, or mental exhaustion and when there is mental exhaustion, there is also physical exhaustion that goes along with it. It's a vicious circle.

Once back up on my feet, I would be charged up ready to fire away again and get to work. But you know what would happen? In another six weeks I would hit burnout again. I would do this repeatedly. Albert Einstein has been credited with this famous quote, 'The definition of insanity is doing the same thing over and over again but, expecting different results.'

Mmm, that *is* insane isn't it? Thinking that working harder and harder, doing the same thing, would give me what I was working towards achieving. Now I did that with everything I put my hand to. My sport, tennis and golf especially, all of my businesses that I had built from nothing, even to training at the gym, learning and studying, everything!

The same pattern over and over again.

It can be scary when you realise it was looking you right in the face but you couldn't see it. I had a definite lack of awareness. I was doing what I thought would be effective, but it was just an endless cycle of staying in the same spot, feeling like I must be getting ahead because I was working so hard, then sitting at a standstill when I hit burnout, then feeling as though I were going backwards and having to start all over again. Crazy stuff!

This is why I share this with you, as you must learn how to manage yourself so that you can work effectively with enormous amounts of motivation, inspiration and energy when needed. And then take downtime at the appropriate times to let yourself recover: spend time with the people you care about most, giving yourself space so you can think and breathe, so that you don't experience burnout and feel as though you are always chasing your tail.

## HAVE YOU EVER EXPERIENCED BURNOUT?

You may have related to the story I shared about having experienced many burnouts.

What about you?

◎

Let's work on you here as I am curious to know if you too have gone through that mental and physical exhaustion of burnout.

Answer these questions in your journal:

⊙   When did you have your last burnout?

⊙   What caused the burnout to occur?

- ⊙ What type of emotions were you going through when you were in burnout mode?

- ⊙ Were there others around you who were affected by your burnout?

- ⊙ How long did your burnout mode last?

- ⊙ How did you get back on your feet and get on with it?

- ⊙ If you look back at other times when you hit burnout, can you see a pattern emerging? Did the same things occur?

What did you discover after answering those questions about your time when you hit burnout?

Working out what your problems are and then how you are going to solve them can be as simple as asking questions of yourself, and coming up with solutions that can become part of your plan.

◎

So now that you are more aware of what happens when you do not manage yourself properly, what are you going to do about it? Because for things to change, you will have to make some changes. Jim Rohn, a pioneer in personal development, said, 'For things to change you have to change.'

As I have said earlier, doing the same things over and over again, working harder and harder, will not be the key to unlocking the power within you. The key will be identifying what the problem is that keeps occurring - that pattern - then figuring out a plan to make changes in your behaviour. You have formed a habit of doing something a particular way, but in order to make the change, you have to develop a new habit, a new pattern of behaviour.

As for my burnouts, I had repeated the same thing for many, many years. I had developed a particular type of behaviour for how to work on achieving my dreams and goals, but struggled to attain them, due to the habits I had developed around working hard. I always felt I never worked hard enough and everything always seemed so hard, but I would keep pushing through the barriers and work harder. But guess what would happen, burnout—burnout—burnout! Remember:

*Burnout = No Energy.*

## HOW TO TACKLE THE BURNOUT AND GAIN MORE ENERGY

When you did the earlier exercise and acknowledged your times of burnout, if you went through the questions, you would have discovered why you hit burnout and most likely you would have seen a common pattern. You have been doing the same thing over and over, correct?

Well, how can we change that? Because in order to really get what we want in our career and in our life, we are going to have to operate ourselves and manage ourselves in a different way.

*A way in which we will be thriving, not surviving!*

We need a plan for you to manage you.

This plan will be part of our overall plan for going after your ultimate dream, but we can get it set up in this chapter to manage you first. Because if you don't look after you first, you can't go after those goals and dreams, simply because you will lack the energy to do so.

There are four foundations that you must have in place to manage you. If you have these four foundations in place, this is your base to build on. In my opinion, if you don't have these basics in place, you will be limited and may not achieve your big-ass dreams. It is not just working on the big dream that will get you there, you need the foundations in place that will be part of your success structure.

## FOUNDATiON 1 – BE iN CONTROL OF YOUR EMOTiONS

You can be in control of your emotions. Most people tend to react and let their emotions take over. They are dictated to by their negative emotional responses to situations, which then affects the rest of their foundations. We can't just have one foundation in place, we must have all of them in place to provide balance and structure to grow.

We talked in a previous chapter about taking control of your emotions. You can decide to be in control. You have the power to make that decision. But you will need to be aware of that decision.

Look around you and see how you respond to certain situations. I am sure you will see there are a number situations that crop up where you react the same way all the time.

Here is an example.

My husband, Ian, beautiful guy that he is, was driving me absolutely nuts with his mobile phone. He had his bluetooth connected to his stereo system in the car so that when a phone call came through, it would come through the speakers loud and clear. At times, technology being technology, and Ian having a bit of a phobia around technology, the car stereo system and the phone didn't always connect. Therefore, when you called him, and the phone hadn't connected with the stereo, you could hear Ian saying 'hello, hello, hello' endlessly when all he had to do was hit speaker mode on his phone. But, because he was not very comfortable around technology, he wasn't sure what to do, even though we had gone through it dozens of times.

Anyway, what was happening with me was this: because we were going through it so many times over the months, I found that each time he rang me, or I rang him and there was no connection between the stereo and the phone, I would be screaming down the phone over the top of his 'hello, hello, hello, hello' voice saying, 'Turn on the speaker on your phone!' It would get to the point I was so aggro (angry), I would hang up on him. He'd ring me back and I would do it again. After we went through that a few times I would be so angry that it would sit with me for another half an hour.

What a waste of energy!

What a waste of time!

I knew I had to change the way I was reacting to it as it simply wasn't serving me well. So, I made the decision to change the way I would respond as I knew this was going to happen repeatedly. When Ian would ring me, with the same issue about the phone, and the endless 'hello, hello, hello' I would just take a few deep breaths, reply with a few 'hellos' back to see if he could hear me, then if not successful, I would hang up, possibly call him again or I would just continue to work on what I was doing at the time. I wouldn't allow myself to get caught up in that emotion of reacting negatively or with anger and frustration. I made the decision to control it.

But you see, something so simple and really trivial when you look at it, can create so much emotion and waste so much energy and time if you are not aware that it is occurring and you don't have a simple strategy in place to deal with it.

I have to share this: at this moment, when I am writing this piece in this book about Ian and his phone, who should call? Yes, you guessed it! Ian! And guess why he was calling me? His phone, his bluetooth, and how they are not connecting with the car stereo. I burst out laughing as soon as he brought it up! Better way to deal with it, wouldn't you agree?

◎

In your journal, write down the answers to the questions below. It will help you work out how you can control your emotions over the things that piss you off!

1.  What are common situations that are really pissing me off right now? (List all of them.)

2.  Why do all of these situations piss me off?

3. Are there any common reactions to these situations?

4. Why am I reacting to these situations?

5. Am I seeing a pattern of reactions to these situations?

6. How long does it take me to recover after I have reacted and become all upset about these situations?

7. Do I believe it is a waste of time and energy?

8. For each situation, how can I respond in a positive way, so that I do not waste energy and emotion on these situations?

Ensure you do this exercise, as it will free you up from wasting emotions, wasting time and wasting energy!

## FOUNDATION 2 – BE IN CONTROL OF YOUR MENTAL STATE (YOUR PSYCHOLOGICAL STATE)

You know, in the last section about controlling your emotions, I discussed with you that you are the ones who makes the decision on how you respond to every situation that comes your way. Well, the same happens here. You make the decisions to be in control of your mental state.

We discussed this in a previous chapter. What you focus on will give you results: positive results or negative results. It will all depend on what you focus on. It is the same here in Foundation 2. It's all about what you are focusing on giving you the results. *Thoughts + Emotions + Actions = Results (Outcome)*.

There is a saying, 'What you focus on expands.' What this means is that the more you think about something, the larger the thoughts become. No matter what it is you are thinking about, the more you think about it, the larger the thoughts become. Whatever you are thinking about emotions are created and you will take actions over what you are thinking and feeling, then you will get a result from that.

For example, back to that tennis match I keep referring to when I played that match and I got wiped off the court, then ran behind the clubhouse and bawled my eyes out. Let's look at that in more detail so you can understand what I am talking about when it comes to being in control of your mental state.

My thoughts

- I had no belief in my abilities.

- I thought I was outclassed.

- I didn't think I was good enough.

- I never believed I could win.

- I didn't want to look like an idiot.

- I didn't want to lose.

- I didn't want to look like a beginner tennis player.

- I kept telling myself I was a loser.

- I kept telling myself I was having myself on thinking I could play tennis.

- I couldn't focus or concentrate.

- My mind was cluttered with thoughts.

## MY EMOTiONS

⊙ I was fearful.

⊙ I was worried about what others thought of me.

⊙ I cried throughout the match.

⊙ I felt humiliated.

⊙ I hated being on the court.

⊙ I felt like I was out of control.

## MY ACTiONS

⊙ I hit most of my service returns either into the net or out of the court.

⊙ I made numerous double faults.

⊙ I had very few rallies back and forth with my opponent.

⊙ I couldn't remember who was serving.

⊙ I had no idea what the point scores were throughout the game.

⊙ I didn't know when to change ends because I kept forgetting the score.

## MY RESULTS (OUTCOME)

⊙ I lost the match.

When we break it down into those four categories of Thoughts, Emotions, Actions and Results we become more aware of what is going on, don't we?

Now that was a negative experience. But what occurs when we have a positive experience? Let's take a look.

In a previous chapter I shared the story with you of when I decided to change my attitude and my thought process to believing that I could hit the golf ball and get feedback, rather than fearing making a mistake with each shot I played.

## MY THOUGHTS

⊙ I believed in me.

⊙ I believed in my golf swing.

⊙ I trusted my decisions.

⊙ I focused one hundred per cent in the present moment.

⊙ I believed I could hit a great shot because I had done the work.

⊙ I knew what to do in each part of the swing.

⊙ When I hit a shot it was just feedback, good or bad.

⊙ I was very clear in my thoughts and my mind was clear.

## MY EMOTIONS

⊙ I was excited about playing my shots.

⊙ I was calm.

- ⊙ I felt in control of my emotions.

- ⊙ I was relaxed.

- ⊙ I was excited about seeing the result of my shots.

- ⊙ I was happy because I was seeing better results.

- ⊙ I felt great and confident about my shots.

## MY ACTiONS

- ⊙ I had a great easy swing rhythm.

- ⊙ I executed more shots with ease.

- ⊙ I was more consistent with my shots.

- ⊙ The balls were going in the direction I planned.

## MY RESULTS

- ⊙ I scored better on the golf course.

- ⊙ I scored better in each area of my golf game.

- ⊙ I had more consistent shots regularly.

This is a much better breakdown: to look at what you can do in a positive experience versus a negative experience. Yet, most people will tend to focus on the negative rather than the positive. They have trained their minds to look at the negatives rather than the positives.

When I have asked clients how they played in their golf competitions, do you know what the responses are? 'I had too many three putts today' or 'I wiped three holes.' When I ask, 'How was the rest of your game, your full swing, chipping, bunker play etc.?' do you know what the response is? They say something like 'Oh, I played great, I felt like my rhythm is better, I felt really great about how I hit this shot, that shot etc., I was really consistent with my chipping and I got out of the bunker on my first shot every time today.'

Why do we look at the negatives first?

Simply because we have made a decision, a subconscious decision, which is something we most likely learned when we were young, that we must look at what the negatives are.

Why not look at the positives?

It is just a switch in your decision making, really in an instant, to focus on the positive things that happen versus the negatives. Of course we have to look at the negatives so that we become more aware of what we need to do to improve, but we should also be aware of the positive experiences and take note of how and why they happen so we can repeat them over and over again.

In your journal, I want you to break down both a positive experience and a negative experience. The reason to do this is to become more aware of:

1. What your thoughts, emotions, actions and results are with a positive experience so that you can repeat it consistently, and

2. What your thoughts, emotions, actions and results are with a negative experience so that you can identify how you respond and what you respond with in order to correct and change your responses into more constructive and encouraging results.

How to write it in your journal:

My Major Negative Experience that really stands out in my mind.

⊙ My Thoughts (write out all of your thoughts).

⊙ My Emotions (write out all of your emotions).

⊙ My Actions (write out all of your actions).

⊙ My Results.

My Major Positive Experience that really stands out in my mind.

⊙ My Thoughts (write out all of your thoughts).

⊙ My Emotions (write out all of your emotions).

⊙ My Actions (write out all of your actions).

⊙ My Results.

You will see by doing these exercises how important it is to be in control of your thoughts and your mental state, as this foundation will be crucial in you achieving your ultimate dreams.

## FOUNDATiON 3 – BE iN CONTROL OF WHAT YOU EAT

You may be thinking, 'Tiff, why do I need to be in control of what I eat, what has food got to do with me achieving my goals and dreams?' I will answer that with the words, 'It has everything to do with you achieving your big-ass dreams!' You will need energy and mental focus to support you in accomplishing what you want. If you don't have energy, you will not have mental focus and therefore you won't attain what you want.

What you put into your body is so important because if you put the wrong type of foods and beverages in your body you will be sluggish and have no energy. You will be tired and drag yourself out of bed. You will just go through the motions to get through the day and you will have lacklustre results. You may put on weight, possibly too much, and be bulging out of your clothes. No dreams can be achieved here.

If you put the right foods and beverages into your body you will feel mentally focused and alert. You will have boundless amounts of energy and your body will love you. You will be able to fit into your clothes. You will feel good about yourself and confident. If you are pursuing a sporting career you will be able to perform so much better.

I will not claim to be an expert in nutrition, but I have enough common sense about it to know what nutritionally benefits your body. There are plenty of food products, food systems and supplements that you can use for that extra edge (all natural). If you want to reach out and have a discussion about what will enhance and progress you forward, by all means I am here for you.

Otherwise, do some research on the internet or in health and nutrition books. There is so much information! It will depend what you want to do and how you want to look after your body's nutritional needs. If you are really struggling and finding it all overwhelming, then work with a dietician. They can guide you and get you on the right path.

When I was younger I never had to worry too much about watching what I ate, because I was very active, a tennis player, a tennis coach and a golf player. I have always eaten the right foods: proteins, vegetables, carbohydrates, good fats etc. but as I was becoming older I noticed I was putting on or carrying a bit of extra weight.

It was really about ten kilograms of extra weight. How did that happen?

It was lack of awareness of what I was putting into my body. I developed a few of my husband's habits. He loves chocolates, lollies and packets of chips. Even though he eats small meals, he doesn't really care too much about eating the foods that will benefit your body. He won't eat vegetables very often - he screws up his face at the thought of eating them - so I have to come up with creative ways for him to eat vegetables. Sounds like the kids, doesn't it?

However, I noticed with myself that I was still eating the way I used to eat when I was a competitive athlete. I ate big servings of vegetables, protein, carbohydrates, good fats but the problem was the snacks I was adding in. It was the few extra chocolates and packets of chips over a few years and then, voila, when I weighed myself and saw myself in a few YouTube videos, I was shocked!

It was easy to let the weight slowly creep on and be none the wiser.

How does the weight creep on? It's the lack of awareness, the lack of paying attention to what you are eating. It's the same issue mentioned in each foundation here in this chapter and in all the other chapters we have discussed and worked through.

The first step will always be creating awareness!

Once I was more aware, I got to work and took off the weight. It took a plan, being in control of my thoughts around food, ensuring that I wasn't going to deprive myself of food that I enjoyed (I have a sweet tooth and I don't believe you should ever deprive yourself), managing myself better with smaller portions and managing my eating habits so that were more beneficial to my body.

You will hear people say, 'As you get older, you will put on weight, that's just what happens,' but if you have my attitude, that is a load of baloney. You can choose, you can make the decision to be whatever you want to be with your weight, it is all in your hands. You are the one who is responsible for your body.

◎

In your journal, write the answers to these questions:

1. Are you aware of what you are eating?

2. Are you eating foods that will give your body the nutrition it needs to perform at its best?

3. What foods do you love to eat?

4. How often are you eating these foods?

5. What are your daily habits eating these foods. Do you eat them a lot throughout the day?

6. What are your weekly habits eating these foods. Do you eat them a lot throughout the week?

7. What foods do you know are good for your body?

8. How often are you eating these foods that are good for your body?

9. What are your daily habits eating these foods. Do you eat them a lot throughout the day?

10. What are your weekly habits eating these foods. Do you eat them a lot throughout the week?

11. Are there areas in which you can improve your eating habits that will benefit your body, your mental focus and energy?

12. Is there anything else that you will need to do around your eating habits?

What have you discovered here about what you eat? Even if you have become more aware that a few changes need to be made, this is all good and positive. Don't be hard on yourself, just keep working on becoming the best version of you that you can be!

## FOUNDATiON 4 – BE iN CONTROL OF YOUR FiTNESS

There will be people who always look after their fitness levels: there are athletes who obviously have to look after their fitness to perform at their best and there will always be people wanting to get fit, but who have that love-hate relationship with it. And you will find that there are people who just don't do anything.

Which ones do you find that suffer the most?

It will be the ones who don't look after their bodies. It will be the ones who don't do anything about their fitness, plus they will be the ones who most likely don't eat right either. Don't let that be you.

It is so important to look after your fitness, for physiological reasons and longevity but also for your mental and emotional state. When you exercise it releases all of these wonderful feel-good chemicals in the brain to assist you in feeling mentally clearer, more focused, alert and energized. It will also leave you feeling good about yourself within, more confident and alive. It's such an amazing sensation nothing that drugs will ever do.

If you are an athlete you understand how important it is to be fit and strong for your sport, but if you are pursuing a different kind of dream, a business dream, a study dream, whatever your dream is, it will also be important to look after your fitness. Never neglect your body. It's the only one you have, so treat it with respect and responsibility.

At times, when you feel that you have to get that task done, that project done, you could be inclined to neglect your fitness because you may feel that your project

or task must be done first before you do anything else. I will always recommend that you don't neglect your fitness regime. The reason for this is it will assist you in having a clearer mind, ready to take on your project with enthusiasm and vigour. And although you may feel a bit sore after exercise, personally I love that feeling because it reminds me I have worked my muscles.

What I love about fitness and health is that the way you look after your body is a true indication of how you operate. Do you have the focus, the tenacity, the mental strength when it gets hard to hang in there or do you just give up? If you do that in your training or fitness regime, it is most likely how you will operate with everything that you approach.

There is a saying, 'How you are with one thing is how you are with everything.' Have a think about it, have you noticed that about yourself?

Remember you are the one who is responsible for your body.

There are a four elements to maintain in your fitness that will benefit you. I have described them below. This is just a quick overview and there are endless amounts of information on the internet and in books about all of this. Don't do just one of these. Introduce all of them into your life. Remember you want to go after this ultimate dream, so do everything you possibly can to give yourself this opportunity. I am encouraging you to have a well-rounded approach to your fitness. *Healthy Body = Healthy Mind.*

## 1. CARDiO FiTNESS

Cardio fitness means cardiovascular fitness, fitness which increases your heart rate. With cardio fitness you want to do exercise that will assist in increasing your stamina. By increasing your stamina you will then be able to focus on your projects for a longer period of time without physical and mental fatigue.

## 2. STRENGTH TRAINING

Strength training is also referred to as resistance training. It is the use of weights or your own body weight to assist you in building your strength. Research indicates that as we age we lose our strength if we don't do anything about it and let the ageing process take over. Fight the ageing process, be strong. Have a strong body. *Strong Body = Strong Mind.*

## 3. HIGH-INTENSITY INTERVAL TRAINING

High-intensity interval training is doing exercises at a high or fast level in a short period of time, or in short bursts. This is amazing training because it teaches you to go hard and fast for a short period of time, raises the heart rate, gets you to sweat and you feel fantastic afterwards. But it's also amazing to help you focus and stay in the moment and give your best effort. Sounds very much like when you are working on the goals you want to achieve in your life, doesn't it?

## 4. STRETCHING OR YOGA

Whether we like it or not, as we get older our bodies stiffen up and the muscles get tight. So we want to ensure that we keep our bodies limber and flexible so that we don't have anything holding us back. Personally, I love yoga for lots of reasons. I love the strength and stability it gives, I love the work on balance to keep that stability and strength in the body, and I love the stretch and suppleness that it gives the body.

What I also love is the focus, staying in the moment, letting go of frustrations and teaching me to do what I can now, to the best of my ability.

In your journal, write the answers to these questions:

1. What days can I incorporate cardio, strength training, high-intensity training and stretching or yoga into my weekly schedule?

2. How often will I do cardio training each week?

3. How often will I do strength training each week?

4. How often will I do high-intensity interval training each week?

5. How often will I stretching or yoga each week?

6. Do I need a trainer, can I do it myself or will I attend classes?

7. What times of the day will I do cardio training, strength training, high-intensity interval training and stretching or yoga?

8. When will I start applying these fitness elements into my week?

# CHAPTER 11

# HOW TO PLAN YOUR ULTiMATE DREAM

*'Setting goals is the first step in turning the invisible*
*into the visible.' – Tony Robbins*

Have you ever set a goal?

We have talked about what it will take for you to achieve your ultimate dream right throughout this book. Did you take the time, after reading the first chapter, to write out what your ultimate dream is, what you really want to achieve in your life? Or is it still in your head even now, but you haven't had the time, nor known how to put your goal into place?

I get it!

You are now well aware of my dream of becoming a world-class tennis player. Number one in the world, not just world-class, the best! You are also well aware that didn't happen, because what held me back was that deep-seated belief that I wasn't good enough.

You know what also held me back?

I didn't have a plan!

I didn't know that I would have to plan how I was going to do it in detail. No one told me. My parents didn't tell me but I don't blame them. They were too busy working, providing for us, giving us a good life, a better life than they had growing up. I didn't learn anything like that at school either. Isn't school supposed to teach you things, to prepare you for the big wide world? All school did, when I was at school, was focus on getting you ready for university. That was the system then. I believe there are changes in the works now, schools offer so much more now than when I was at school, but do they get you ready for the world?

I will leave that answer in your court!

Years later when I was finishing my last year of university, I had to figure out what I was going to do. What would I do with a Human Movement degree?

When you start asking yourself questions, your mind starts looking for the answers.

The answer came to me to create a business teaching sports skills to kids. I was already teaching tennis to kids as a part-time job whilst going through uni, but I saw a need for sports skills in our changing world. Kids were playing less sport, and doing more indoor activities like computer games or Nintendo. The iPhone hadn't been invented yet, but we had mobiles, and kids' ball skills were deteriorating.

I grew up when computers didn't exist. Well they were starting to appear but no one I knew had one, let a alone a mobile. That's right it was the 1980s, we had colour television (which was a big deal) and a landline telephone. The internet didn't exist and our entertainment was to climb trees, play sport or ride your billycart throughout town. Fun times!

How was I going to create this business?

I had no clue. I knew what to teach and how to teach the skills, that wasn't the issue. It was how to get the business off the ground. What would I need to do?

You know the answer, it's to write out a plan.

I won't bore you with the details of the plan, but it was a very successful business and I was very proud of what I had created from nothing.

## WHY YOU MUST HAVE A PLAN

You may be thinking, 'Tiff, I know what I am doing, I've got this, I don't need a plan, I have my dream.' Yes that is right, you do have your dream, which is so awesome.

But in order for us to turn it into a reality, we have to map out how you are going to get there.

Even for me to write this book, I had to plan it out. I had to work out why I wanted to write this book, who I was writing this book for, how I would lay out each chapter, what I would write about in each chapter. Then I had to work out in my schedule when I was going to write it, how much time I was going to dedicate each day to writing it, when I was going to have it completed. Then I had to stick to the plan to get it done by the date I had set for it.

Now before we actually get to the part where we are going to work together writing out your plan, let me say that it's important to have a deadline to get things done. But what happens if you don't get it done in that time frame?

I will put it this way. Just say you are working on your big-ass dream of competing at the Olympics. It is four years away, and this is it! You have to do all the physical training, the mind training, eat right, be coached and do everything you need to do to achieve this dream of qualifying for the Olympics. You have your deadline set.

And you don't qualify. You miss selection by two places. You were almost there but not quite.

Are you a failure? NO!

Should you give up on your dream?

NO WAY!

Sometimes it will take longer to get to your dream than originally planned. But YOU DON'T GIVE UP! You just keep going until you get there no matter how long it takes.

I taught golf to a lady called Sue a few years ago. Now she had a goal that by the end of January she would achieve a 30 handicap. She had just started playing competition the previous year off a 45 handicap. At the beginning of January she had a meltdown, even though she was only two shots off reaching 30. She felt as though she wasn't going to make it by the end of January.

Sue didn't break her handicap of 30 by the end of January, she did it seven months later. Now why do I tell you this story?

Sue didn't give up on her goal. Sure, it took longer than planned, it was harder to break through than she had thought. It wasn't just the training, it was having her mind in the right mental state each time she practised and played competitions, but she did it. She didn't give up, she kept going until she got there.

DON'T YOU GIVE UP ON YOU!

But you must plan out what you want. When you have a plan you know what action steps you must be taking. You know what you must be doing each day. You have drive, you have purpose, you are focused.

When you don't have a plan, you are distracted, lost, frustrated, overwhelmed, questioning whether you should even be working towards this dream, thinking things such as, 'Is it really going to happen anyway?'

Are you with me?

Are you ready to start working on your plan?

All you need to say is, 'Yes Tiff, I am in!'

Let's begin!

## THE PLAN FOR YOUR ULiTMATE DREAM

Benjamin Franklin said, 'If you are failing to plan, you are planning to fail'.

There are numerous ways to set goals and ways to write up a plan: you can download them off the internet. However, I am going to share with you what works for me. It will be the attention to detail that will make all the difference.

I cannot stress enough how important it will be for you to plan out how you are going to achieve your ultimate dream. As mentioned before, if you don't plan you will lose direction and lose faith. You will lose sight of your vision and get distracted. You will get frustrated, be angry and upset. You may even lose interest, veer down another path and before you know it, you will be doing something completely different. You will then ask the question, 'How did I get here?'

# GOAL – PURPOSE – STRATEGY (GPS)

To plan out your dream we are going to use a strategy known as GPS that is; Goal - Purpose - Strategy. GPS in technology today is known as the Global Positioning System. What we are doing with this GPS strategy is to position you in the world with where you want to go and what you want to do. This system will be your plan.

I love this form of goal setting. We can get clear on what you want, why you want it and how you are going to get it.

## GOAL (WHAT DO I WANT?)

This is our first part of your plan, 'What Do I Want?'

Don't get too concerned about the detail yet, we will get to that. We talked about your big-ass dream in the first chapter, what you want, so let's write it out here now in your journal!

*My ultimate dream is*_____

## PURPOSE (WHY DO I WANT IT?)

This is the second part of your plan, 'Why Do I Want It?'

We need to know why you want to do what you have set out to do in your world. This will be what will drive you, because when you find things getting tough, hard and frustrating, feeling like you just want to give up—and you will—you will have to revert back to 'Why Do I Want It' and remind yourself of why you are going after your ultimate dream.

Just wanting that dream will not be enough, unless we can emotionally connect you to why you want the dream in detail.

We are about to commence planning out your ultimate dream. I want to make you aware that Steps 1, 2 and 3 are designed to clarify where you are currently, we can call this your current reality. Once you have completed Steps 1, 2 and 3 we move onto Steps 4 to 12, to map out your ultimate dream.

Get out your journal and let's begin the Twelve Steps to Planning Your Ultimate Dream.

### STEP 1: WHAT DON'T I HAVE RIGHT NOW IN MY LIFE AND WHY DON'T I HAVE IT?

I want you to write out in detail what you don't have. Why haven't you achieved your big-ass dream yet? Why are you disappointed with yourself? Why are you letting yourself down? Are you letting your family down? Why?

Write it out in detail, I want you to get really upset, really pissed off with yourself.

### STEP 2: WHAT HAVE I LEARNED UP TO THIS POINT IN MY LIFE?

There are three areas in this question I want you to write about and to become more aware of. These three areas we will be working on are:

1. When you were successful.

2. When you were unsuccessful.

3. What lessons you have learned.

#### WHERE HAVE I BEEN SUCCESSFUL?

Write out how you have been successful. What has contributed to that success? What habits did you apply? What was your work ethic like? Were

you focused? Did you plan it out? Did you schedule when you had to do it? The more detail, the more you can understand how you operate in success mode.

### WHERE HAVE I BEEN UNSUCCESSFUL?

Write out here where you have been unsuccessful. It's perfectly fine to be unsuccessful at things, we all have been. This is how we learn about what not to do. What did you feel here that contributed to you not being successful? Let's see what comes up for you here.

### WHAT HAVE I LEARNED?

This is where you write out everything that you have learned along the way: all the lessons you have learned. It is lessons learned that worked and lessons learned that didn't work. This is to get a better understanding of howfar you have come and how open you are to the lessons you are learning, so that we can work towards the future that you want.

## STEP 3: DESIGNiNG YOU INC.

Here, in designing YOU INC., we are going to get clear on your vision, who you want to become.

1. Describe who you want to become.

   Who is it that you want to become? What type of person do you want to be? What are your values? What are your standards? What do you expect from yourself each day? How should you operate each day? How do you treat yourself and others around you? Are you respectful? Do you have a role model? How do they operate? What type of standards do they set for themselves on a daily basis?

2. What is your purpose?

What do you feel your purpose is? What are you meant to do here on this planet? What type of difference do you want to make to you, to your family, to your friends, to your tribe, to the world? We all feel that we are here for a reason, what is your reason?

## STEP 4: THE BiG FiVE

What are the 'Big Five'? The Big Five are the five big moves you need to take in order to accomplish your big-ass dream. Now we don't need to detail each of the five big moves yet, we will do that in the next few steps. But what we need to do is work out what the five important moves are.

I will use the example of writing this book and then you can apply what I have shared to work out your Big Five!

What I suggest here is to work backwards, as it will be easier to figure out your starting point.

Here's an example of working backwards:

1. Finish writing the book.

2. Write the chapters.

3. Plan out what to write in each chapter.

4. Schedule when I will work on writing the book.

5. Plan when I want the book finished by.

Now if we flip it around you will see that we have worked out the Big Five in the order we want to write and complete the book, starting with the deadline, then working out the planning and scheduling, then the writing.

When I learned to set up each goal this way—create the Big Five, then work backwards to get the steps in place, it made achieving the goal much easier.

Now, it's your turn. Write out the Big Five to achieve your ultimate dream!

Have you written out the Big Five? Do not continue to the next step until you have completed this one, as you will need this step to get closer to actioning your ultimate dream.

### STEP 5: HOW LONG WILL THE BIG FIVE TAKE?

In this step we need to work out how long it is going to take you to accomplish these five big moves. For the purposes of showing you how to map out your finish date, goal date and completion date for your ultimate dream, using the five big moves, I have used an example of a sports person who wants to compete at the Olympics. You may not be a sports person or have aspirations to compete at the Olympics, but use this information to help you get clearer in identifying your five big moves:

1. Compete at Olympics.

2. Qualify at national selections for Olympic Team.

3. Compete at World Titles.

4. Compete at National Titles.

5. Compete at State Titles.

Now if we flip it around we have:

1. Compete at State Titles.

2. Compete at National Titles.

3. Compete at World Titles.

4. Qualify at national selections for Olympic Team.

5. Compete at Olympics.

We now have the Big Five in place.

Then we need to find out when the Olympics is held, the year and month, and we map that out on your calendar.

From the date the Olympics is held, we then work backwards and discover when each of the other events is being held and map those dates out in the calendar. Now you may not have all the dates and details for those yet, but work it out roughly as this will help you with your preparation.

Let's recap here. We should have the dates for when these events are on over the next four years, so that we can put an action plan in place for each.

## STEP 6: CREATE YOUR ACTION PLAN FOR YOUR NUMBER ONE MOVE OF THE BiG FiVE

Now, because the Olympics is four years in the future, there is much to do to get there. What you can control right now is creating your action plan for your number-one move of the Big Five. In order for you to get to the Olympics you will need to achieve this one first.

It's awesome to have the ultimate dream of going to the Olympics, but unless we have a plan in place for each step, then we can't make it happen.

Here in Step 6, we need to do the Big Five again, but only for your first goal, whatever that number-one move was. In this example we are using the 'compete at the state titles'.

What are your Big Five for the state titles? Let's work it out together backwards.

1.  Compete at State Titles.

2.  Ease off training before State Titles.

3.  Find competitions to practice competing in pressure situations.

4.  Training for your sport.

5.  Find a coach.

What we have identified are your five most important steps to achieving this first part of your big-ass dream.

Again, we have to get out the calendar and work out when the state titles are on. Once we know the date, this is what we do next:

1.  Write the date in your calendar.

2.  Figure out how many days until the State Titles.

3.  Figure out the days that are rest days.

What we have is:

*Days Until State Titles – Rest Days = Amount of Days for Training and Competitions*

*e.g. 180 days – 24 rest days = 156 days*

*The 156 days is what you have for training and competitions.*

Now work out how many days you have for competition.

*Days Available For Training and Competition – Competition Days = Days Available For Training*

*e.g. 156 days – 24 days = 132 days.*

*What that gives you is 132 days left for training.*

With your calendar, you can now map out:

1.  The twenty-four rest days that you will have.

2.  The twenty-four competition days.

3.  The days that you will be training (132 days for training).

You may find this difficult to do, all this planning stuff. But, I guarantee the preparation is in the planning and you will get the results that you want if you put the detail in here now.

What your training consists of and how you train will be what you will figure out with your coach. So now we will flip your Big Five around so that you can see the sequence of steps that need to be taken in order for you to achieve your number-one move of your big-ass dream!

1.  Find a coach.

2.  Training for your sport.

3.  Find competitions to practise competing in pressure situations.

4.  Ease off training before State Titles.

5.  Compete at State Titles.

What we have worked out:

⊙ When you will be competing at the State Titles.

⊙ When you have rest days.

⊙ When you have competition days.

⊙ When you have training days.

These are all mapped out in your schedule for the next 180 days leading up to the state titles or that number-one move of the Big Five you have planned for your big-ass dream.

Remember this is just an example for you, but you can apply this to whatever your ultimate dream is, whether it be sport, a business, a promotion at work, anything that you are working towards.

## STEP 7: LEARN AND WORK ON YOUR SKiLLS

In this step you want to identify the skills you need to be learning and refining to help you achieve the number-one move of your big-ass dream.

1.  Write out all the skills you need to learn and refine to help you achieve your first goal (your number-one move towards your ultimate dream).

2. Which skills are the most important, the skills that you must focus on currently to assist you in accomplishing your number-one move? Choose no more than five skills.

3. With these five skills you have discovered, what do you need to know or do so that you can master those five skills? Write out each skill and the points which identify what you need to learn in detail about that skill.

Once you have accomplished your number-one move of your ultimate dream, then you can repeat this process for your number-two to number-five moves, in learning and working on your skills.

## STEP 8: IDENTIFYING YOUR STANDARDS AND VALUES

We discussed your standards and values in Chapter 9, Mental Focus and Controlling Your Emotions. You would have done the exercise and listed out your standards and values already, and we want integrate them here.

The questions following are here to remind you so that you can add in your standards and values in this section.

⊙ What are my standards, my daily modes of operation? What do I expect from myself and how do I conduct myself?

⊙ What are my values? What do I value that is important to me so that I become the person I am striving to become?

## STEP 9: PROBLEMS OR OBSTACLES

In this section, we refer to the problems or obstacles that you believe you will encounter. I would love to tell you that everything will be smooth sailing and you won't encounter any challenges along the way, but you will.

We talked about this in Chapter 6, *The Obstacles You Will Face*, and you encountered and identified obstacles that you had faced or are facing. What we want to do here in Step 9 is detect what obstacles you envisage and then create a plan in this section for how to deal with them when you encounter them.

Let's focus here though on your number-one big move. Your number-one big move will be the first part of your ultimate dream that you will tackle, so let's focus on this one. You can repeat this process for each challenge that you encounter along the way.

⊙ What challenges do I see that I will encounter for my number-one big move? List them all.

⊙ For each challenge, recognize what the challenge is, then ask why it is a challenge. Keep asking why they are a challenges until you see what the root of the challenge is.

⊙ Once you have detected the obstacles of the challenge, what type of action steps are you going to put in place so that you won't be held back by that challenge when it occurs?

Let's clarify.

1. What is the challenge or obstacle?

2. Why is it a challenge or obstacle?

3. What is the plan I need in place to overcome the challenge or obstacle?

## STEP 10: WHO ARE MY ROLE MODELS?

You want to have role models. These are people that have 'made it' in your eyes. These people have achieved what you would love to accomplish. Write down:

1. Who are my role models?

2. What is it that I admire most about them?

3. What are their standards and values?

4. How do I learn from them?

Use your role models as inspiration to keep striving towards your ultimate dreams.

## STEP 11: MY GPS PLAN FOR MY ULTIMATE DREAM

Following is a simple template that you can copy. It's a matter of seeing it all on one sheet. You can put it on the wall above your desk, somewhere you can see it every day. This template is for you to use to achieve your ultimate dream.

| GOAL (G) | PURPOSE (P) | STRATEGY (S) |
|---|---|---|
| **WHAT DO I WANT?** (What is my ultimate dream?) In this section you write out what your ultimate dream is. Also share here who your role models are that will inspire you to achieve your ultimate dream. | **WHY DO I WANT IT?** (Why do I want my ultimate dream?) In this section you write out all the reasons why you want to achieve this ultimate dream and the consequences if you don't achieve it. | **HOW DO I GET IT?** (How am I going to get my ultimate dream?) In this section you write out what you are going to do to achieve your ultimate dream. Write out your action steps, your Big Five moves. |

## STEP 12: MY GPS PLAN FOR MY NUMBER-ONE BiG MOVE

This template is for you to take action now on your ultimate dream. We worked out earlier in Step 6 what your number-one big move is for you to take action on. Again, once you have filled this out, stick it up on your wall above your desk, take a photo of it, put it on your phone as the wallpaper so that you can see it every day. You want it to remind you of what you are focusing on right now to achieve this first part of your ultimate dream.

| GOAL (G) | PURPOSE (P) | STRATEGY (S) |
|---|---|---|
| **WHAT DO I WANT?**<br>(What is my number-one big move?)<br><br>In this section you write out what your first big move is of your ultimate dream.<br><br>Also share here who your role models are that will inspire you to achieve your<br><br>ultimate dream. | **WHY DO I WANT IT?**<br>(Why do I want this number-one big move?)<br><br>In this section you write out all the reasons why you want this number-one big move to happen and the consequences if you don't make it happen . | **HOW DO I GET IT?**<br>(How am I going to achieve this number-one big move?)<br><br>In this section you write out what you are going to do to achieve your number-one big move.<br><br>Write out your action steps. |

## STEP 13: YOUR TiME iS NOW

Step 13 is the most important step that you will need to take. It is time to get started on your dream today and take action. You have put all the steps in place to begin, therefore your time is now.

It is time to begin!

# DREAM BIG.
# BELIEVE IN YOU.
# GO AFTER YOUR
# DREAMS!

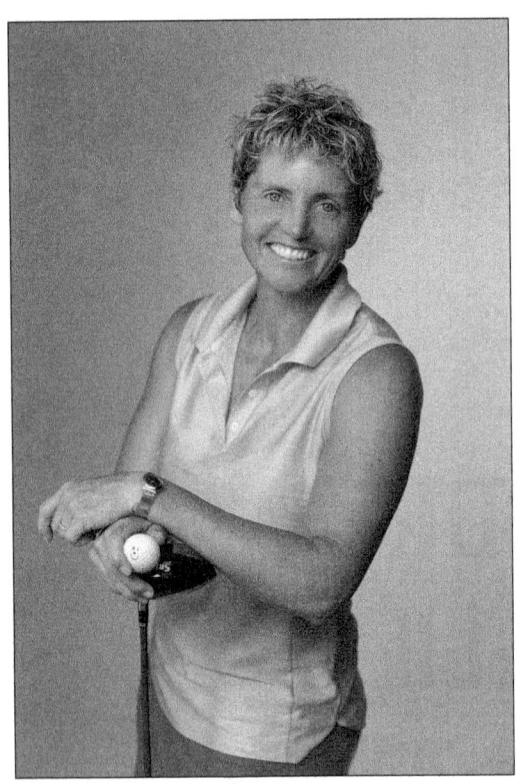

## ABOUT TiFFANY MiKA

As a young woman, Tiffany Mika dreamed of an international professional tennis career. Today Tiff is a sought after coach and mentor, and founder of Reach Your Potential with Tiff, and The Lady Golf Teacher. She has a degree in Human Movement Studies and is a professional sports teacher with over 20 years experience coaching tennis and golf. Tiffany Mika is also a highly regarded speaker.

## WORK WITH TIFFANY MIKA

**Email:** tiff@tiffany-mika.com

**Web:** www.tiffany-mika.com

**Facebook:** www.facebook.com/tiffanymikatakesaction

**Instagram:** www.instagram.com/tiffanymikacox

**Twitter:** twitter.com/TiffanyMika